LIFE RENOVATION

A Faith-Based Blueprint
for Renewing Every
Area of Your Life

LIZE LANDIS

To

Jaime, Katelyn and Taylor
My three greatest gifts and joys of my life. You are the
motivation behind every decision I make. Love you all
endlessly. Grateful to be your Mom.

And to the love of my life, **Gregg**
I would not want to build a life, or renovate a life with
anyone else. You are my absolute favorite! I love you.
Grateful to be your Wife

First Edition: 2026

ISBN: 979-8-9947567-0-6 (Soft Cover)
ISBN: 979-8-9947567-1-3 (E-Book)

Printed in the United States of America
Marigold Press

Cover Design by Dakota Weber

Table of Contents

INTRODUCTION

Welcome to Your Life Renovation

Have you ever stood in a room in your house and thought, *"Wow, this room really needs an update!"* Maybe it's your kitchen. The appliances are outdated, the cabinets are falling apart, and nothing quite works the way it's supposed to. You might have a deep desire to cook amazing meals for your family, but you simply can't do that with a kitchen in this condition.

Or maybe it's your bedroom. The comforter on the bed is old, full of holes, and decorated with a pattern you despise. The furniture doesn't match, and somehow the room has become a dumping ground for clutter from all over the house. You dream of the bedrooms you see in magazines; spaces that are calm, inviting, organized, and peaceful. A place that feels like an escape, not a burden.

And then there's the attic or storage room; you can barely open the door. Piles of stuff are stacked everywhere. Most of it is junk, but somewhere buried in the chaos are a few precious items, memories and keepsakes that you can't even enjoy because they're lost in the mess.

But what if someone told you your entire house could be fully renovated - transformed into everything you've ever dreamed of?

What if you could have:

- A gourmet kitchen with the latest technology, new backsplash, stunning lighting, and cabinetry that works like a dream?
- A bedroom that truly feels like a retreat; organized, peaceful, and beautiful?
- A storage room that's decluttered, purposeful, and even pleasant to walk into?

Now, imagine if you felt the same way about your life.

What if you could walk through your life like you walk through your home - room by room, space by space and assess what needs to change?

What would you find?

Would you dread entering certain areas; places in your heart and mind that you've given up on or tried to avoid?

Are there spaces you simply survive in but deeply wish were different?

When you look at your relationship with your spouse, do you feel:

- Safe?
- Content?
- Joyful?

Is your marriage a place you retreat to when you need rest from the world, or has it become just another disordered, overwhelming room with holes in the walls and emotions dumped on the floor?

- What about your baggage?
- Are you still walking through life carrying the weight of past wounds, disappointments, and unhealed pain?
- Have you been holding onto things for so long that you can't even imagine what life would be like without them?

Maybe you've forgotten how to dream. Maybe you've stopped believing that transformation is possible.

But here's the truth: **your life can be renovated.**

Just like a home, your life can be restored, refreshed, and reimagined.

- You can identify the broken spaces.
- You can discover what's outdated, what's missing, and what needs to go.
- You can rebuild on a strong foundation, filled with purpose, peace, and hope.

And the best part? **You don't have to do it alone.**

This book is your blueprint. Your guide. Your invitation to step into the process of life renovation.

Together, we'll walk room by room; through your
heart, your habits, your relationships, your faith,
your dreams, and you'll be handed the tools to
rebuild.

So, take a deep breath. You don't have to have it all
figured out. You just have to be willing to begin.

Take one room at a time. You might spend months
in one chapter, or you might get through four
chapters in a day. There is no timeline, but there is
purpose.

Let today be the start of your renovation journey.
Not just for your home. For your life.

What is The State of Your Home?

*"Unless the Lord builds the house, the builders
labor in vain."*
 - Psalm 127:1

Renovating your life and marriage begins with an
honest look at where you are. No blueprints, no
paint swatches, just truth. Because, before you can
rebuild, you must know what's broken.

Maybe life has felt like it's crumbling. Or maybe just
a few rooms are messy, and you've ignored them
long enough. Either way, this first step is about
seeing clearly.

It's time to assess:

What is the current state of your home and your life?

Start with asking yourself these 6 Questions:

1. What Is the State of Your Home?

Take a moment to reflect. Which description below best matches your life right now?

A. The Entire House Was Destroyed

Maybe a crisis hit like a hurricane. Infidelity. Financial collapse. A devastating diagnosis. The emotional structure of your life has caved in. The foundation may still exist somewhere under the rubble, but the damage is massive and overwhelming.

This stage feels hopeless. Devastating. But even here, rebuilding is possible if you're willing to clear the debris and begin again.

B. The House Is Still Standing, But Most Rooms Need Renovation

You're holding it together, but barely. Your relationship with your kids might be okay, but your marriage is dry. You feel distant from God. You look around and ask, "How did I get here?"

You don't need to bulldoze the entire structure, but most rooms need work. A lot of work.

C. One Essential Room (Bathroom, Bedroom, Kitchen and Living Room) Is Outdated and Affects Everything Else

Sometimes, a single neglected area (like emotional health or spiritual connection) throws off the rest. One toxic habit, one broken pattern, one unspoken hurt can spread like mold through the rest of your house.

The good news? Addressing that key room can transform the entire home.

D. The House Is Doing Pretty Well, But There's Always Room for Improvement

Maybe you're doing okay, but "okay" isn't your goal. You want vibrancy, connection, purpose. If this is you, praise God. But stay open. Renovation isn't just about repairing damage, it's about preparing for beauty.

E. You Don't Even Know What a House Is Supposed to Look Like

You didn't grow up with healthy models. You're not sure what's "normal" or "good." That's okay. This book will walk you step-by-step through God's design for a spiritually healthy, emotionally thriving home.

2. What Does My Dream House Look Like?

God gave you the ability to **dream**. So many people stop believing things can be different. Don't let your past define the future.

A. Allow Yourself to Dream

What do you long for? Peace in your home? Connection with your spouse? Laughter with your kids? Deeper intimacy with God?

God is the architect of redemption. He makes beauty from ashes.

B. Realize That Change Is Always Possible

It's not too late. No matter how long it's been broken, no matter who failed whom, renovation is possible.

3. How Much Will This Cost?

A. God Will Ask Something of You

"If anyone would come after me, let him deny himself and take up his cross daily and follow me. For whoever would save his life will lose it, but whoever loses his life for my sake will save it." - Luke 9:23–24

Renovation costs something. God will ask you to **trust Him**. To **obey**. To **surrender** your pride. To **forgive**. To **persevere**.

B. It Will Cost Time, Energy, and Commitment

"I am the light of the world. Whoever follows me will not walk in darkness, but will have the light of life." - John 8:12

You can't microwave transformation. Renovation takes time. But every moment is worth it.

C. What's the Cost of Doing Nothing?

Sometimes it's easy to say "no" to a renovation because the cost seems too high and the time commitment seems too big. However, the more important question would be, "What if we leave it as is"? The hard truth is that if you don't renovate, the house will keep falling apart. The rot will spread. Destruction is inevitable if neglected long enough.

<u>4. Who Do I Need to Hire?</u>

You were never meant to do this alone, and in just the same way that we need to hire different experts when we renovate our home, we need experts when we renovate our lives, too!

"If you call out for insight and raise your voice for understanding… then you will understand the fear of the Lord and find the knowledge of God." - Proverbs 2:3–7

A. Architect – GOD

He holds the blueprint. Trust His design.

B. Builder – COUNSELORS & MENTORS

God often uses people to help build what we cannot build alone.

C. Subcontractors – FRIENDS, FAMILY, SUPPORT NETWORK

Find people who speak life, truth, and encouragement over your journey.

5. What Are the Steps to Complete the Renovation?

A. Demolition – Some walls must come down.

B. Dig Deep – Check the foundation. Is Christ really at the center?

C. Overcome Obstacles – Remove what's blocking growth.

D. Installation – Bring in new habits, thoughts, and patterns.

E. Finishing Touches – Add grace, joy, and beauty.

F. Maintenance – Keep walking with God. Keep showing up for each other.

6. How Long Will This Take?

Every renovation is different. The key is to **stay on track**.

Commit to the process. Progress, not perfection. That's what we'll walk through together.

What We'll Cover in Each Chapter

Each part of this book will focus on a "room" in your house;each representing a part of your spiritual and relational life.

In every chapter, we will explore:

- **What does this room represent?**
- **What is your personal responsibility in this room?**
- **What does God's Word say about this area of your life?**
- **What practical tools will help you renovate it?**

Now it's time to get real - and I would suggest if you are married that you each do this assessment separately. Be honest with yourself as you assess the different areas of your life.

There is no wrong answer.

In fact, the more honest you are the more successful the renovation will be. This is also a starting point to have a real conversation with your spouse about where they think things are at.

Maybe you think you have a good grip on your family mission - but your spouse feels lost and disconnected. Maybe your spouse feels like parenting is going well, and you feel at your wits end when it comes to taking care of children.

So take a few HONEST minutes and rate the different areas of your "home".

Home Assessment Tool

Take inventory. Rate each area of your home/life from 1 (disaster) to 5 (strong).

<u>*Area of Life/Home*</u>   **Rating (1–5)**

Design (Hope for something new)

Foundation (Relationship with Christ)

Bathroom (Understanding self)

Kitchen (Emotional, physical and spiritual health)

Master Bedroom (Intimacy/Rest)

Family Room (Your family mission, and the heart of your home)

Children's Rooms (Parenting)

Office (Work-life balance)

Dining Room/Guest Room (Fellowship & influence)

Design (Hope for something new)

Foundation (Relationship with Christ)

Bathroom (Understanding self)

Kitchen (Emotional, physical and spiritual health)

Master Bedroom (Intimacy/Rest)

Family Room (Your family mission, and the heart of your home)

Children's Rooms (Parenting)

Office (Work-life balance)

Dining Room/Guest Room (Fellowship & influence)

Part 1

FOUNDATION

CHAPTER 1

Laying the Foundation - Building a Life That Stands

"You can't build a home without a foundation."

That's where we begin. Whether you're newly married, rebuilding a relationship, or simply trying to strengthen your life from the ground up, the first step is always the same: *build on a solid foundation.*

As mentioned in the introduction, each section, we'll explore a different "room" of the house; a metaphor for key areas of life and marriage. These rooms represent different aspects of who we are and how we connect with others: communication, intimacy, purpose, finances, spiritual life, and more. But before we start renovating any of those spaces, we must ask: **What is the house built on?**

Without the right foundation, no matter how beautiful the rooms, the structure won't stand.

Now let's talk about the foundation itself. We're not diving into the "rooms" just yet. Instead, we're going to dig deep into the very ground your life and marriage is built on.

Think about it: if your life is in ruins, if your relationship is struggling or undergoing a rebuild, the foundation determines everything. Without a strong base, any attempt to renovate or improve other areas will eventually crumble. I love analogies (as you'll learn quickly).

Picture a beautiful home with a gorgeous kitchen and perfect furniture; if that house is built on cracked concrete or shifting sand, eventually those beautiful rooms will be swallowed up by instability. You'll see cracks in the walls. You'll feel the imbalance. The collapse may not come overnight, but it will come. The same is true in marriage, family, and life.

What Is the Foundation?

As believers, this foundation is **God**. It is His Word, His truth, His presence. Everything else we discuss in this book is built upon this.

I know this personally. Many years ago we went through a very dark time in our marriage, when things had completely fallen apart. We didn't find healing through a shelf full of marriage books. We found it in **scripture**. We found it **on our knees**. We found it in who God is; not just who we wanted Him to be, but who He reveals Himself to be in His Word. If we're going to build a life that lasts, we must build it on God's truth - not opinions, not trends, not self-help hacks. We must root ourselves in something unshakable.

Wisdom or Foolishness: The Rock or the Sand

Let's start with a familiar image; maybe one you remember from childhood. Remember the song about the wise man who built his house upon the rock?

Well, it comes straight from scripture:

"Therefore everyone who hears these words of mine and puts them into practice is like a wise man who built his house on the rock.

The rain came down, the streams rose, and the winds blew and beat against that house; yet it did not fall, because it had its foundation on the rock.

But everyone who hears these words of mine and does not put them into practice is like a foolish man who built his house on sand.

The rain came down, the streams rose, and the winds blew and beat against that house, and it fell with a great crash."
(Matthew 7:24–27)

You can hear the words. You can know the verses. You can even sing the kids' song. But unless you **put them into practice**, you're building on sand. And when the storm comes, the crash will be devastating. I remember seeing a reel of a magnificent home on a hill overlooking the ocean; it was everything you would think a house should look like, and I'm sure the people living in that home were the envy of their friends. However, the reel then showed a landslide coming down, and in just a few minutes the entire house was destroyed and disappeared under the rubble. I just kept staring at it thinking how quickly that can happen. But guess what was NOT on that hill - a solid foundation. It was not built on rock! What an incredible reminder of the importance of a solid rock foundation!

Our God: The Rock That Doesn't Move

Throughout scripture, God is described as a rock; immovable, solid, a place of refuge.

Here are just a few reminders:

"For who is God besides the Lord?
And who is the Rock except our God?
It is God who arms me with strength and keeps my way secure.
He makes my feet like the feet of a deer;
he causes me to stand on the heights."
2 Samuel 22:32–34

Let's pause on that last line: "He makes my feet like the feet of a deer."

It might sound odd at first. But dig deeper. Deer are not known for strength; they're not lions or bears. But their feet are uniquely designed to navigate rocky mountainsides. They can leap, balance, and climb in places few others can reach. That's not because they're powerful, but because they're equipped. God made them that way.

And He makes **you** that way too.

God Is Our Fortress

"But the Lord has become my fortress, and my God the rock in whom I take refuge." Psalm 94:22

This isn't just a poetic line, it's a promise. A fortress shelters you when the storm hits. When everything else feels unstable, God does not move.

Nothing Can Separate Us

Perhaps the most powerful foundation verse of all is found in Romans:

"In all these things we are more than conquerors through Him who loved us. For I am convinced that neither death nor life, neither angels nor demons, neither the present nor the future, nor any powers, neither height nor depth, nor anything else in all creation, will be able to separate us from the love of God that is in Christ Jesus our Lord."
Romans 8:37-39

This is where we start.

Before the renovation.

Before the planning.

Before the communication tools and date night ideas and parenting tips.

We start here, with an unshakable truth: **God's love holds you, secures you, and cannot be taken from you.**

Your First Step

So here's your first tool:

1. **Ask yourself: What is my life built on?**
2. **Meditate on these scriptures. Read them out loud. Use them as your prayers.**
3. **Invite God to be the foundation - not just in words, but in practice.**

Before we move on to the rooms of the house; before we tackle intimacy, connection, trust, or routines; we need to pour concrete. Let God be your rock.

The rest of the house depends on it.

So, Who God Is? - The Foundation of Everything

In any room of married couples, there's a wide range of experiences; some are thriving, some are barely holding on, and most fall somewhere in between. But regardless of where a marriage stands, there's a truth that applies to every person: your personal foundation must be built on the character of God. Without that, no marriage, or life, can be truly strong.

This chapter shifts the focus from "we" to "me," because before we can build a solid partnership, we must know, trust, and walk with the God who created us, understanding who God is. His character, His love, His presence, is not just foundational – it's transformational.

Now, imagine a young boy who dreams of being an NBA star. He's talented, but he doesn't have access to coaching, camps, or even his own basketball. One day, someone offers him a chance of a lifetime: Michael Jordan, the greatest basketball player of all time, will come live with him – training him, coaching him, and mentoring him every step of the way. He'll even answer questions the boy doesn't know he should be asking. Can you imagine if this boy said, "No thanks, I'm good, I think I can figure this out on my own." ABSOLUTELY NOT! He would jump at the opportunity!. Now imagine for a second that after he said yes, he just let Michael Jordan sit in his house for a year and did not interact with him at all. Not once. That would be insane.

Now, I know it's a wild scenario, but it helps illustrate something even greater. We don't have Michael Jordan in our living room; we DO have God. The God of the universe, who made us, knows us, and loves us, is sitting on the couch beside us every day. And yet so often we ignore Him, walking past Him in the chaos of our lives, surprised that things feel messy or disconnected.

God isn't an occasional advisor. He is everything. But we need to recognize who He is and actually invite Him into the conversation. He knows the answers to EVERY area of our lives. He already knows what tomorrow is going to look like and how

we are going to handle it. Why are we not seeking
His advice ALL DAY LONG?

Chapter 1 *Reflection Questions*:

1. What is your life currently built on? When storms come (stress, conflict, or unexpected challenges), how stable is your foundation?
2. In what ways have you relied on self-help strategies, trends, or human wisdom instead of grounding your life and marriage in God's truth? How has that worked out for you?
3. Reflect on the metaphor of the wise man building his house on the rock. What practical steps can you take to "build on the rock" in your daily life and relationships?
4. How do you invite God into the details of your life on a daily basis? Are there areas where you've been ignoring His presence or guidance, like the scenario of letting Michael Jordan sit silently in your house?
5. Considering God as your unshakable foundation, how might your perspective on marriage, parenting, and personal growth change if you consistently rooted your decisions, priorities, and emotions in His character and love?

CHAPTER 2

God's Resume

Let's pause and reflect on God's resume. Not as a theoretical concept, but as a reality we can live into. We often turn to Him when things fall apart or give Him casual thanks when things go well. But who is He really? Let's look at a few key truths:

1. God Is Creator - When You Feel Unknown

Genesis 1:1 says, *"In the beginning, God created the heavens and the earth."*

God didn't just show up later to fix things; He **made** everything. He knows how it all fits together. He's not guessing about your life; He crafted it. Luke 12:7 reminds us that *"even the hairs of your head are all numbered."* That's how intimately He knows you.

If you've ever created something, even a simple, imperfect craft, you know it well. You know where it might fall apart. You know the design. God knows you more deeply than that, because you are His creation.

2. God Is Love - When You Feel Unloved

It's easy to feel unloved in this world; in our marriages, workplaces, even churches. But God doesn't just show love; *He is love.*

1 John 4:8 says, *"Whoever does not love does not know God, because God is love."*

That means love is not just what He does, it's <u>who He is</u>. You don't have to earn His love or wonder if it's real. His very nature is the definition of love, and it never wavers.

3. God Is Good - When the World Feels Dark

When life feels unjust or full of hardship, it's easy to question if God is truly good. But 2 Peter 1:3-4 tells us that God's divine power *"has given us everything we need for a godly life"* and that we can *"participate in the divine nature, having escaped the corruption in the world."*

God doesn't ask us to spectate. He invites us to participate. He gives us His goodness, His promises, and the strength to live a holy life even in a broken world.

4. God Is Our Guide - When You Feel Lost

Life is full of crossroads, parenting challenges, job changes, financial strain, and health crises. We often feel unsure which way to go. But Psalm 48:14 assures us: *"For this God is our God for ever and ever; he will be our guide even to the end."*

We don't have to rely on our own logic or emotion. In fact, that often leads us the wrong way. God's guidance is steady, wise, and available;if we ask.

5. God Is All-Knowing - When You Don't Know What Comes Next

Jeremiah 29:11 is a verse many know by heart: *"'For I know the plans I have for you,' declares the Lord, 'plans to prosper you and not to harm you, plans to give you a hope and a future.'"*

This isn't just a feel-good phrase, it's a deep truth. God knows what lies ahead. He isn't surprised by your fears or confused by your path. Matthew 6:8 adds, *"Your Father knows what you need before you ask him."*

6. God Sees You - Even When You Fall Quietly

I remember when our daughter was young and still did gymnastics. She did a routine and fell in front of all the other kids. She quickly stood up, said she was fine, and smiled through what was clearly pain and embarrassment. As her mother, I could see the truth behind the brave face.

That's how God sees us. We fall and tell ourselves, and everyone else, we're fine. But God knows the hidden hurt. He doesn't need a polished explanation. He already understands, and He's already offering comfort.

Afterwards, we got in the car, and I turned to her and said, "Hey, I'm really proud of you. You kind of kept it together back there. I saw you fall and hit your head. I could tell you wanted to cry. You always say, 'It's fine, it's fine, it's fine,' even when you want to cry," I said gently.

She looked at me, eyes wide and sincere, and whispered, "How do you know me so well?" I smiled and asked, "Was I right?" She nodded quickly. "Oh

yes. I totally wanted to cry. But I just told myself, 'If I talk myself through this moment, I can hold it together.'"
 She laughed. "I really thought I fooled everyone, even you." I told her, "But I'm your mom. I see you."

It wasn't magic. It wasn't even a superpower. It was simply presence. I'm there every day. I hear her thoughts as she shares them with me. I see her try and fall and try again. I know her patterns, her insecurities, her brave face. That's how I knew.

And then it hit me. Matthew 6:8: *"Do not be like them, for your Father knows what you need before you ask him."*

If I can know my child that well, how much more does the Father know us?

He sees us fall. He sees the way we smile while blinking back tears. He knows when our lives look perfect on the outside but are falling apart on the inside. He sees beyond the painted walls of our hearts to the cracked foundation no one else notices.

Psalm 139 says:
"O Lord, you have searched me, and you know me. You know when I sit and when I rise; you perceive my thoughts from afar."

That verse humbles me every time I read it. The thought that God knows my thoughts, before I speak them, before I try to clean them up is a little scary. Think about how judgmental or harsh or self-critical our thoughts can be. Yet He sees it all, and still He stays.

He knows us. Deeply. And completely.

He Calls the Stars by Name

"He determines the number of the stars and calls them each by name." Psalm 147:4

When I was around twelve years old, we lived in Namibia, on the western coast of Africa. It's a land of high dunes and vast desert, bordered by ocean and sky. One year, Halley's Comet passed by, and we camped in the middle of the desert to see it. Far from any city lights, deep in quiet sand dunes.

Lying there on my back, I saw stars like I had never seen them before. No distractions, no buildings, no noise; just a canopy of constellations stretching endlessly across the sky. The stars weren't just a handful of twinkling dots like we often see in cities. They were countless, blazing, and beautiful.

And God, Scripture says, *knows each one by name.*

In that moment, I thought: If He knows the names of stars, burning balls of gas light-years away, how much more must He know my name? My needs? My heart?!

That's the God we're talking about. He's not just mighty. He's intimate. Personal. Present.

7. God is Sovereign

Sometimes life makes us feel powerless. We try to
control things, and they slip through our fingers.
We plan, we pray, we prepare, and yet, life spins in
ways we never expected.

But the sovereignty of God brings comfort.

Colossians 1:15–18 tells us:
*"The Son is the image of the invisible God, the
firstborn over all creation. For in him all things
were created... all things have been created
through him and for him. He is before all things,
and in him all things hold together."*

There's something so steadying about those words:
"in him all things hold together." When everything
feels like it's unraveling, He holds. When we lose
our grip, He never loses His.

He is not only the beginning - He is the glue in the
middle and the victor at the end. And He chose, in
His supreme authority, to give us life through
Christ.

Colossians 2:13–14 says, *"When you were dead in
your sins... God made you alive with Christ. He
forgave us all our sins, having canceled the written
code... He took it away, nailing it to the cross."*

We were lost. Destined for death. But God changed
it all with one decision: to send His Son. And that
decision changed everything.

8. God is Faithful

I remember clinging to Deuteronomy 7:9 during one of the darkest seasons of my life:

"Know, therefore, that the Lord your God is God; He is the faithful God, keeping His covenant of love..."

Eighteen years ago, our marriage hit the breaking point. We had reached a crisis point and the realization that we were at rock bottom was heart breaking. My idea of what marriage was supposed to be was shattered. My heart was broken. My trust in our relationship was destroyed. The world as I knew it had cracked wide open.

But even in that pain, I learned something about God: He doesn't leave...

Not when we fall.
Not when we fail.
Not when we feel most unlovable.

Night after night, I lay with that verse in my heart: *He is faithful.*

Not just to the good parts of us. But to all of us.

If you have ever felt abandoned; by a parent, a friend or even your spouse; know this: God will never leave your side. You can scream, cry, push Him away... and He will stay. He will never break His covenant promise to you. He will remain faithful, always.

9. God is Gracious

Guilt has a way of creeping into the corners of our lives. Sometimes it's over big things. But often, it's in the small things; moments in marriage or parenting when we make each other feel small or wrong.

We make our spouse feel guilty for a night out, or for needing a break, or for wanting something that brings joy.

Galatians 5:1 reminds us:
"It is for freedom that Christ has set us free. Stand firm, then, and do not let yourselves be burdened again by a yoke of slavery."

Guilt can feel like a heavy chain. A chain that should not exist. Are we able to use what makes us feel guilty as a guide to see where change might be needed, sure. But it should not be something we hold onto and keep as a chain around our hearts. Christ broke that chain. He doesn't bind us with shame. He frees us to walk forward.

I would like to note here that shame is very different from guilt. We often interchange them, but it's incredibly important to understand that they are not the same. With guilt we have that feeling of "I DID something wrong" - it's an action word, and therefore if something wrong was done, there can be repentance and things can be fixed. There is a motivation for change. With shame we believe the narrative that "WE are defective". This is a core issue of self and can be incredibly destructive. It will allow us to spiral, feel defeated and not motivate us to change.

Grace means you don't have to carry the weight of guilt OR of shame!.

10. God Is Unchanging

When life feels uncertain, shifting, or unstable, we can rest in the unchanging nature of God. Psalm 33:11–13 reassures us:

"But the plans of the Lord stand firm forever,
the purposes of his heart through all generations.
Blessed is the nation whose God is the Lord,
the people he chose for his inheritance.
From heaven the Lord looks down
and sees all mankind."

God's plans are not fickle. They are firm. His purposes do not expire or adjust with the culture or with our behavior. And as His children, we are part of that plan;chosen, seen, and secure.

Philippians 1:6 echoes this steadfast promise:

"Being confident of this, that He who began a good work in you
will carry it on to completion until the day of
Christ Jesus."

God does not start something in you and then give up. He is consistent and committed;yesterday, today, and forever.

11. God Is Forgiving

Guilt is one of the enemy's favorite tools. If he can get you to sit down in shame, he can take you out of the game entirely. But guilt and shame have no place in the heart of someone who belongs to Christ.

Second Corinthians 5:17–19 reminds us:

"Therefore, if anyone is in Christ, he is a new creation:
The old has gone, the new has come!
All this is from God, who reconciled us to himself through Christ and gave us the ministry of reconciliation: that God was reconciling the world to himself in Christ, not counting people's sins against them."

You are not disqualified. Your past is not a barrier. That's the beauty of the cross - your sin is paid for, your shame is washed away. When guilt creeps in, bring it to the light. Surround yourself with community. Root yourself in truth. Speak out loud what's real and push back against the lies.

12. God Is Merciful

Titus 3:3–7 captures our story, all of us:

"At one time we too were foolish, disobedient, deceived and enslaved by all kinds of passions and pleasures. We lived in malice and envy, being hated and hating one another.
But when the kindness and love of God our Savior appeared,

he saved us, not because of righteous things we had done,
but because of his mercy."

That mercy has nothing to do with how good we are and everything to do with how good He is. He saved us through the Holy Spirit, poured out generously. We are heirs. We belong. Even when we feel lost, mercy finds us.

13. God Is Our Provider

When everything seems to be unraveling; when your job disappears, your relationship hits a wall, or life just feels empty, remember this promise from Philippians 4:19:

"And my God will meet all your needs according to the riches of his glory in Christ Jesus."

Not just your basic needs. Not from scarcity. From glory. From His endless resources.

Notice the verse says needs, not wants. This requires trust. God may not always provide what we *want*, but He never fails to provide what we *need*. So, surrender your desires to Him. Ask Him to align your heart with His. Trust that He is already working on your behalf.

14. God Is Long-Suffering

We all have moments where we feel like we just can't get it right. We fall into the same pattern again, say the same words we didn't mean, or respond from old wounds. But even in our repetition, God does not abandon us.

"For the Lord your God is a merciful God; He will not abandon or destroy you or forget the covenant with your ancestors,
which he confirmed to them by oath." Deuteronomy 4:31

God doesn't give up on us. He's not going anywhere. So don't sideline Him. Don't treat Him like a distant advisor. He's like Michael Jordan on the couch; ready to play. Invite Him in. Get in the game with Him.

So REMEMBER …..

These scriptures aren't just encouraging; they're *powerful tools*. One of the best things you can do is take these verses and put them on notecards. Carry them with you. Post them on your mirror. Keep them where you'll see them.

Because when emotions hit, when Satan whispers lies like, "You're unloved" or "You're alone," you need something to fight back with. That's what God's Word does. When you read a card that says, *"God is love"* and it's backed by scripture, it realigns you with truth.

Talk to God. Ask Him questions. Let Him guide you. Don't let the world or your emotions define reality. Let God's Word do that.

Now that we've reminded ourselves of who God is, we also need to be alert to who Satan is, and how he works. Because while God is always present, so is the threat of erosion.

We're about to dive into the next section: the *cracks in the foundation*. No marriage, no individual, is immune. And often, it's not the big, dramatic cracks that destroy a structure. It's the countless tiny fractures, the slow decay, the subtle shifts.

You may think, "That's just a small thing," but small things compound. Forty or fifty small cracks – resentments, distractions, unmet expectations – can suddenly collapse the whole thing when pressure hits.

So, before we talk about rebuilding or reinforcing, we must understand what causes those cracks. And most of all, we must remember this:

God is on the couch, ready.

Are you inviting Him into the game?

1. How often do you turn to God only when things fall apart or when life is inconvenient? How might your relationship with Him change if you actively invite Him into every part of your day?
2. Reflect on the different aspects of God described here: Creator, Love, Goodness, Guide, All-Knowing, and more. Which of these truths do you most need to remind yourself of right now, and why?
3. Think about moments when you tried to handle life on your own. How might trusting God as your guide, provider, and fortress change the way you approach challenges?
4. In what ways do you allow guilt, shame, or fear to overshadow God's grace, mercy, and faithfulness in your life? How can you intentionally remind yourself of His promises in these moments?
5. God sees you, even when no one else does! He knows your heart completely. How does this reality affect the way you view yourself, your decisions, and your relationships with others?

CHAPTER 3

Knowing Your Enemy and Guarding Your Heart

There's a dangerous place we can slip into spiritually, and it sounds something like this: "I've got it all together. I don't need to talk to God today." But let me tell you - that's exactly when the enemy sees an opening. If you're not turning to God, guess who steps in? Satan. And he's more than ready to convince you that you need him instead. Don't be fooled. If you've grown complacent or distracted, he seizes that moment to slip in and plant his lies.

Just in case you're unclear about who Satan is, Scripture lays it out plainly. First Peter 5:8 warns us:

"Be self-controlled and alert. Your enemy the devil prowls around like a roaring lion looking for someone to devour."

I grew up in South Africa, and no, we didn't have lions casually roaming our neighborhoods! But South Africa does have a game park called Kruger National Park, which is the size of a small U.S. state. You can drive through it and see the wild animals in their natural habitat. When I was younger, our family vacationed there. On one of the days, we were able to witness a lion kill and then sat in the car watching the aftermath. We stayed for hours, watching the circle of life unfold; lions feasting, hyenas waiting their turn, and vultures circling. It was brutal, raw, and unforgettable.

And here's what struck me: lions are patient. They wait. They watch. They don't grow bored and leave if nothing happens right away. They wait for the tiniest sign of weakness; when an animal lowers its head to drink, even if its ears are up. That's when they strike. It's not quick or merciful. It's bloody. It's painful. And that's exactly how Satan operates. He waits for you to be distracted, emotionally vulnerable, or spiritually distant. Then he attacks. Not to inconvenience you but to destroy you. He doesn't go easy. He goes for maximum pain. And the aftermath is pure destruction!

"He will cause deceit to prosper, and he will consider himself superior. When they feel secure, he will destroy many."
Daniel 8:25

Satan considers himself superior. But let's be clear: <u>he's not</u>. ***God is superior.*** Satan just wants you to believe otherwise.

Matthew 24:24 warns us:

"False Christs and false prophets will appear and perform great signs and miracles to deceive even the elect, if that were possible."

We are surrounded by these false prophets. Instagram filters present a perfect life. Facebook feeds show highlight reels of family bliss. Social media paints a picture of perfection that is often far from the truth. And it messes with our perspective. Even well-meaning friends or coworkers may influence us with worldly advice that feels helpful but isn't grounded in God's truth. That's what Scripture means by false prophets; people who appear trustworthy but are (sometimes unknowingly) pulling us away from God's voice.

"Watch out for false prophets. They come to you in sheep's clothing, but inwardly they are ferocious wolves." Matthew 7:15

And Satan? He can use anything and anyone – a friend, a movie, a social media post, even someone in your closest circle – to whisper lies or sow doubt. He uses whatever door you leave open.

"But I am afraid that just as Eve was deceived by the serpent's cunning, your minds may somehow be led astray from your sincere and pure devotion to Christ." 2 Corinthians 11:3

You only get led astray when you lose focus. When you're walking closely with God, focused on His presence, it's a lot harder for the enemy to deceive you. If you start drifting, if you stop talking to God, that's when Satan moves in.

John 10:10 puts it plainly:

"The thief comes only to steal and kill and destroy; I have come that they may have life, and have it to the full."

Satan is a thief. He wants to rob you of peace, of joy, of purpose. And he waits for a crack in your foundation, just a moment of weakness, to slip in and steal what God has planted.

In South Africa, home break-ins are common, so people install burglar bars - not just on windows, but between sections inside the house. Why? To stop thieves from reaching the bedrooms, where the family sleeps. We understand the need for that kind of protection at home. But what about in our spiritual lives? Are you building those same burglar bars around your heart and mind? Are you guarding your thought life, your emotions, your relationships — the places where the enemy can sneak in? Satan is not omnipotent. He's not the Creator. He didn't make you. God did. That means Satan doesn't own you. You have a choice. You can say, "No. You don't get access to my mind today."

When Triggers Invite the Enemy In

Let's talk about one of Satan's most effective weapons: *triggers*.

These are emotional buttons that, when pushed, send us into a tailspin. We all have them.

A trigger is anything that makes you react with negative emotion: maybe with anger, defensiveness, insecurity, or withdrawal. Sometimes you lash out. Sometimes you shut down. And you might not even realize why.

There are two types of triggers:

1. **Lifelong Triggers** - formed in childhood or through repeated experiences.
2. **Circumstantial Triggers** - tied to specific situations or seasons.

Let me give you an example from my own life.

Since my dad was in the military, I moved a lot as a child. I never got used to being the "new kid." Deep down, I longed for stability, longed to live in one town, go to one school, have one set of lifelong friends. But that wasn't my story. So that constant feeling of being the "new kid" often caused me to feel insecure and out of place.

As an adult, I still carry that trigger. When we moved to Florida, I dreaded the thought of entering new social circles, joining a new church, and once again being "the outsider." I can be outgoing and confident. But stepping into a room for the first time where relationships between the people are already established? That sends me into a silent panic. How does this impact my emotions at home? It means that for days leading up to a new group event, I'm on edge. I second-guess myself. I get snappy. I criticize my husband or become impatient with the kids; not because they've done anything wrong, but because I'm fighting an inner storm. In the past, that caused tension, confusion and arguments.

Once I was able to see that trigger for what it was and how Satan was effectively using it to create a crack in our home foundation - I realized the importance of making my husband, Gregg, fully aware of what actually happens inside my emotions and why. Now that he understands this trigger, he doesn't take my mood personally. He leans in. He fills my mind and heart with truth all week long.

"You've got this."
"They're going to love you."
"And if they don't? I love you."
"You're enough. You're seen. You're secure."

His encouragement helps anchor me before the storm hits. He reminds me that the lies Satan whispers, including, "You won't fit in," "You'll be rejected," "You're too much, or not enough," are just that - lies.

Now let's talk about circumstantial triggers

A **circumstantial trigger** is a short-term environmental stressor that wears you down slowly until suddenly, you're ready to lose it over a sock.

A day-to-day circumstantial trigger for me is related to my home. This was especially evident when my kids were little. I generally like to keep a tidy house. It brings me a sense of calm. But with three kids, I've learned that chaos is often part of the package deal. For a few days, I let chaos slide. I ignore the clutter. I tell myself, *Don't stress them out. Be flexible.* But then that internal pressure builds.

That's when I know I need to communicate my trigger before it explodes. So I'll go to my husband, Gregg, and say something like:

"Hey babe, just letting you know, at some point today, I need this house tidy. I'm not sure how it's going to happen, but could you please step in and give some instructions, because I'm done. I've asked in every tone and tense of the English language, and nothing's changing."

Twenty years ago, Gregg would have responded with something like:

"Lize, they're just little kids. Who cares? You're totally overreacting. No one's coming over. It's fine."

But the thing is, I cared. I didn't need anyone else to care. I didn't need company to justify my emotional need. I just needed some family effort to restore a bit of peace. I needed to sit in the bliss of order. Maybe for my husband to take the kids outside for a bit, so I could enjoy the rare serenity. Today, he gets it. He recognizes this as one of my circumstantial triggers. Instead of criticizing or dismissing, he now partners with me. He'll step in, gather the kids, crank up the music, and start delegating:

"Okay, who's got the living room? Who's on shoe patrol? Let's get this place cleaned up!"

Suddenly, we're a team. I feel seen, heard, and supported; not criticized or crazy. He even affirms me:

"Well done for not freaking out for four days. I'm proud of you."

Such a simple change. But it's created a dynamic shift.

Understanding my trigger, and Gregg responding with partnership instead of pushback, turns what could have been a meltdown into a moment of connection.

Gregg has triggers too. One of his lifelong ones? Being told *no* or *what to do*.

In his words:

"If you tell me no, I'm probably going to try and do it anyway. If you tell me what to do, I instinctively want to do the opposite. It's just how I'm wired. It's probably why I run my own business!"

It took time for me to recognize this in him. But now, I understand how that kind of control or restriction hits a nerve for him. So, when there's something we need to talk through, whether it's about work or family decisions, I've learned to approach it with more awareness and care. Sometimes I even step in protectively and help him recognize the trigger before it blows up into something bigger.

And then there's **the food trigger.** (Yes, food.)

Gregg is a go-with-the-flow kind of guy... until he's hungry and has a craving. And when that craving is for pizza, but the family decides on Panera, let's just say, he's not great at letting it go. We've had entire evenings derailed because we went to Panera while Gregg spent the meal daydreaming (out loud) about Pizzeria Uno.

"We could've gone to Pizzeria Uno. The kids would've liked it. The pizza's better there…"

He'll keep poking the topic, and I'll eventually snap: "You know what? Forget it! Let's just go to your stupid pizza place. I hope they mess up your order. I hope you choke on your pepperoni." (Don't judge me. You've been there too.) But again, over time, we've grown. Now we have conversations like:

"Hey babe, are you really feeling like pizza tonight?"

"Yeah, I'm craving it."

"Okay, then let's go."

Or…

"No, I'm fine with Panera, but I was just throwing it out there."

"Okay, good, then please don't mention Pizzeria Uno again tonight or my attitude is going to significantly shift."

We joke about it now. We've learned to name the trigger and talk about it proactively. And that one change has saved many evenings and date nights. Because honestly, it's not the big things that usually break us. It's the little ones. These small, repeated moments of misunderstanding or dismissiveness that chip away at intimacy and connection. Recognizing the "stupid little things" and responding with compassion makes all the difference.

Here is a list of common emotional triggers. It's not exhaustive, but it's a helpful place to start. As you read through, don't just look for the words that describe you, look for their **opposites**.

Ask yourself:

- How do I feel when I'm disrespected?
- How do I react when things are chaotic?
- What emotions arise when I feel misunderstood, unappreciated, or controlled?

If the reaction is strong, there's a good chance you've just found one of your triggers.

Once you name it, you can talk about it. You can protect each other around it. You can become partners instead of opponents in those difficult moments.

You can become a team:

Feeling:

accepted

understood

in control

that you have his attention

peaceful

ordered

safe

like you are fun (or can have fun)

respected

needed

right

comforted

balanced

like there is variety in your relationship/life

like your relationship/life is predictable

challenged

liked

valued

fairly treated

like you have freedom

there is consistency

loved

included

autonomous

How Triggers Affect You - and Everyone Around You

Triggers are not just personal, they are relational. They impact how we feel, how we react, and most importantly, how others experience us.

When you're triggered, you're the first to feel it: the flood of emotions, the tightness in your chest, the surge of defensiveness or withdrawal. But don't be fooled into thinking the impact stops with you. Triggers create relational ripples that reach far beyond your own internal world. Imagine your spouse walking into the house and having to emotionally brace themselves, wondering, *"Is this the moment I get hit?"* It's not a physical hit. It's the emotional whiplash that comes from negative energy, sharp words, or cold withdrawal. Unlike when you play "pie in the face" and get hit in the face, a moment of laughter you post on Instagram, this kind of hit leaves no smiles, only emotional wounds.

And it's not just your spouse. Your kids, your co-workers, even the driver in front of you can get swept up in the wake of your unacknowledged triggers. When we don't deal with our internal reactivity, it spills into our relationships, our home atmosphere, and even our spiritual vitality.

So what do we do?

Step One: Recognize the Trigger

Before we can heal, we have to notice our triggers.
Begin with curiosity:

- *Why am I reacting this way?*
- *What was said or done that set me off?*
- *What do I believe in this moment that is fueling this reaction?*

Spend the next month becoming a student of your own reactions. Whether it's your spouse leaving dishes out again, your child back-talking, or that car in front of you driving 10 miles under the speed limit, when you feel that internal flare-up, pause. Observe. Take note.

And write it down.

As you begin to name your triggers, you will start to reclaim your power. Triggers lose their grip when they're no longer operating in the shadows. Awareness opens the door to transformation.

"Be self-controlled and alert. Your enemy the devil prowls around like a roaring lion looking for someone to devour."
1 Peter 5:8

I will be covering Step Two and Step Three in detail in Chapters 5 and 6!

Chapter 3 *Reflection Questions*:

1. In what areas of my life am I most likely to become spiritually complacent, and how might that create openings for the enemy?
2. Which personal triggers, lifelong or circumstantial, most often influence my reactions, and how do they affect my relationships at home, work, or church?
3. How aware am I of the subtle ways Satan might use people, social media, or circumstances to sow doubt or distraction in my life?
4. What practical steps can I take to "guard my heart" and protect my thoughts, emotions, and relationships from being exploited by the enemy?
5. How can I partner with my spouse, friends, or community to recognize and respond to triggers in ways that create connection rather than conflict?

CHAPTER 4

Start Building your God-Centered Foundation

In the next part of our journey, we're going to dive deeper into self-awareness. We'll explore who you are, not just in relation to your spouse or family, but in the eyes of God. Who did He design you to be - apart from anyone else's choices, failures, or approval?

This is step one. Pay attention to your triggers. Notice. Name. Write. Pray. Begin the sacred work of becoming reacquainted with yourself and with your Creator.

Once we begin to acknowledge and work through our triggers, something beautiful happens: we make room to dream again. You get to actually start imagining what a life would look like that is everything you might have dreamed of.

The Power of a God-Centered Foundation

When your house has a firm foundation (Christ) everything changes. That doesn't mean the house is finished or the rooms are renovated. But it does mean you can begin building again, one step at a time.

And what better place to start than dreaming?

"May the God of hope fill you with all joy and peace as you trust in him, so that you may overflow with hope by the power of the Holy Spirit." Romans 15:13

The key phrase is *"as you trust in him."* Hope grows in the soil of trust. If you want to overflow with hope, it starts with placing your trust fully in God. And from that trust comes courage;not fear. The spirit God gave us is one of power, love, and self-discipline (2 Timothy 1:7).

So, shake off the fear. You were made to dream.

Let the Pages Be Written, But by Whom?

Your life is a book with blank pages ahead. The past is written, today is happening;but the future is still unwritten. Who will write it?

If you don't write it intentionally, someone else will. The world will. Your circumstances will. Satan certainly has drafts ready to fill in the blanks;with fear, shame, failure, or apathy.

So we return to God's Word:

"Now to Him who is able to do immeasurably more than all we ask or imagine, according to His power that is at work within us..." Ephesians 3:20

Even if you're in crisis, if your dream feels shattered, or your hope lost, God's dreams for you haven't stopped. He can do more than you could ever ask for. Even when you sit in a pile of disappointment and say, *"There's nothing left to dream about,"* God whispers back, *"I'm not done yet."*

Let His voice be louder than the doubts.

Counting the Cost: To Dream or Not to Dream

Dreaming isn't cheap.

There's a cost to daring to believe again:

- It might be uncomfortable.
- You might fail.
- People might not understand.

But there's a greater cost if you don't.

Think of the movie *Field of Dreams*. Ray Kinsella stood at the crossroads of a decision: sign the papers and give up on the dream, or risk everything and hold on. If he had quit, generations would have lost something beautiful.

Your dreams matter. Not just for you, but for your family, your marriage, your legacy.

There is always a cost to renovation. It takes time and energy, and sometimes it's messy. But if you don't do the work? The house will crumble or never be transformed into what it could be. The same is true of your soul, your marriage, and your dreams.

"But we have this treasure in jars of clay to show that this all-surpassing power is from God and not from us. We are hard pressed on every side, but not crushed; perplexed, but not in despair; persecuted, but not abandoned; struck down, but not destroyed." 2 Corinthians 4:7-9

Yes, we will be pressed. But we are not without power. We may be struck down, but we are not destroyed. The world will tell you to give up, to settle for mediocrity or walk away. But God calls us to more.

So what's your dream?

What blank page do you need to start writing on again?

Don't sign the papers. Don't give up. The people are coming, the field will be filled, but only if you dare to believe that with God, there's still more ahead.

Holding Fast to Hope: Strength for the Journey

In 2 Corinthians 4:16-18, Paul writes:

"Therefore, we do not lose heart. Though outwardly we are wasting away, yet inwardly we are being renewed day by day. For our light and momentary troubles are achieving for us an eternal glory that far outweighs them all. So we fix our eyes not on what is seen, but on what is unseen, since what is seen is temporary, but what is unseen is eternal."

Yes, troubles and hardships come. Life can be hard – physically, emotionally, and spiritually. But these moments are not meaningless. They are shaping something eternal. When we look through the lens of eternity, our daily struggles take on a new meaning. They become the refining fire preparing us for glory far beyond what we can imagine.

This perspective invites us to count our trials as joy, knowing God is at work even in the hard times. The key is to *look up*;not just at what's pressing down on us, but at the eternal hope ahead.

Pressing Forward: Forgetting What Lies Behind

Philippians 3:12-14 has been a lifeline for many:

"Not that I have already obtained all this, or have already been made perfect, but I press on to take hold of that for which Christ Jesus took hold of me. Brothers and sisters, I do not consider myself yet to have taken hold of it. But one thing I do: Forgetting what is behind and straining toward what is ahead, I press on toward the goal to win the prize for which God has called me heavenward in Christ Jesus."

We don't need to have it all figured out. In fact, Paul admits he's still pressing on, still growing, still striving. What matters is the attitude of perseverance. Forget the failures, the pain, the disappointments. Press on toward the goal. Day by day, step by step, keep moving forward.

If you're in the muck right now, this is your encouragement. You don't have to have the answers today, just the determination to keep moving toward the life God is calling you to.

Protecting Your Dreams from Dream Stealers

One of the most powerful lessons is this: *Don't let anyone steal your dreams.*

Sometimes dream crushers aren't strangers or random people, they are the closest people in your life. A spouse, a family member, a friend, or even a boss may, intentionally or unintentionally, try to diminish your hopes.

Your dreams are God-given and a part of your unique purpose. Protect them fiercely. Hold fast to the vision God has planted in your heart. Recognize when negativity from others is trying to pull you down, and learn how to set healthy boundaries to guard your hope.

As the motivational message from the movie *The Pursuit of Happyness* reminds us:

"Don't let anybody tell you you can't do something - not even me. You've got a dream, you have to protect it."

The Power to Do All Things

Philippians 4:13 boldly declares, *"I can do all things through Him who gives me strength."*

This isn't about relying on your own power, your spouse's encouragement, or your friends' support alone. The strength to face every challenge, pursue every dream, and rebuild every broken piece comes from God.

This verse forms the foundation of our hope and action. It reminds us that we are not alone in the struggle or the dreaming. God's strength empowers us to do the impossible.

Building a New Foundation

Your time has come - starting today. Lay that foundation. If cracks start occurring, face them and fill them.

Building on this new, unshakable foundation allows miraculous transformation. With God's strength and guidance, no renovation is impossible.

So, pick up the ball, step onto the court, and play your part. Dream boldly. Build courageously. Trust the strength God supplies.

Before we enter into the next chapters of this book I want to pause a moment and give you an opportunity to DREAM.

If your foundation has been set - it's time to start dreaming of what your house is going to look like. Sometimes it's hard to dream when you don't even know what a great house would look like. But imagine - in much the same way as building an actual house - things you might have seen or heard about. A large wrap-around front porch, or maybe a pool in the back yard. You might not know every detail, but you do know what it would feel like to live in a dream house. The amazing thing is that God wants you to live in a home and marriage that exceeds your expectations! So, step away from your reality right now and realize you have an endless budget. Dream.

Practical Steps: Dreaming with Purpose

Now that you've been reminded of hope and strength, you may be wondering, *"What do I do next? How do I start dreaming again?"*

Everyone's starting point looks different:

- Maybe you never learned how to dream because it wasn't modeled in your family.
- Maybe you feel stuck in a place so hard that getting out of bed is a victory.
- Or maybe you're already living your dream, but you want to grow deeper.

No matter where you are, the first step is the same: *get clear on who you are.*

In the next section of this book we will explore practical ways to discover your true self, who God created you to be, and how that shapes your needs and your marriage.

Start building the "Job Description" and "Resume" of Your Marriage

I have worked in both the corporate and non-profit worlds. And regardless, in business, you don't apply for a job without a clear job description. You know what's expected, you prepare your resume, and you go for it. If there are areas of the job description you might not know, you make sure you learn them quickly and are willing to be taught.

Marriage needs the same clarity.

Do you know your spouse's "job description" – what they need from you in order to feel loved and supported? Do they know yours?

These "job descriptions" need to be clearly defined. I remember my husband, Gregg, asking me years ago what he could do that afternoon to make my day better. Without hesitation I said "grab me a Starbucks". So you know what he did - he went to starbucks and got me a Hot Chocolate (which is my favorite "hot" drink). Well guess what? I was actually disappointed when he arrived with the drink. That seems crazy, right? Well, it was a hot day and when I asked for the Starbucks I had visualized an iced chai and had been so excited for the refreshing drink. So, when the hot chocolate arrived all I could think about was that he had not fulfilled what I really wanted.

Whose fault was it? Had he done what I had originally asked? Absolutely. However, I had not defined what I really meant. So instead of feeling grateful, I felt annoyed and that, in turn, made him frustrated. How crazy that if I had simply clarified or if he had simply asked for more clarification - it would have been a different outcome.

If there is anything I would hope for you to take away from reading this book, it would be the importance of defining. DEFINE, DEFINE, DEFINE. Keep asking questions until there is no more clarification needed.

Dreaming Your Marriage into Reality

When it comes to your marriage, I want you to begin by putting words on the page that describe your dream marriage. Maybe you're already living in that dream! Fantastic! Write down how you're feeling today. But if you aren't there yet, don't worry. Instead, write down the way you wish you were feeling.

I often hear from couples, especially from wives, something like: *"I don't even know how to dream."* Many came from childhood homes where love was chaotic or absent. One might say, *"I grew up in a broken home where my parents argued all the time, so I don't even know what I should be asking for."*

If that's you, start with what you do know - your feelings. For example, if you find yourself thinking, *"I don't feel seen right now,"* then write down the word **seen**. If you feel small or unappreciated, then write down **appreciated** or **acknowledged**. Your current negative feelings, though painful, are powerful clues pointing toward what your heart truly needs.

Step One: List Your Words

I want you to do two important things.

First, gather words that describe how you want your marriage to feel. It could be five words or fifty words, the number doesn't matter. What matters is that you keep adding to this list throughout your life because your needs and dreams will grow and change.

Examples of words could be "loved, seen, protected ..."

Step Two: Seek God's Word on Your Words

Next, don't just stop with writing down the words. This month, I challenge you to go deeper and explore what God says about each word. Instead of giving you a long list of verses, I want you to become a seeker of truth. Look up scripture for each word on your list. For example, if **loved** is on your list, search the Bible for what God says about being loved. Write down the verses, meditate on them, and write out the passages if you can.

If what you are hoping "love" will feel like aligns with how God describes it in scripture - I can say with FULL certainty that if both you and your spouse desire God's definition and put the work in - that it WILL happen. This is not only an exercise in what YOU want your spouse to do for you - but equally importantly - how to do these things for your spouse.

Why? Because before you can build a solid marriage, you have to build on a solid foundation: the Word of God. Your "job description" as a spouse isn't just a list you make up; it's God's calling and design for your life and your marriage.

Keep this list of words and accompanying verses - because in those moments when it's hard to do the work, pull the list out and remember what you are working towards!

Can you imagine what it will feel like to sit in a relationship where all these words are true to your life?!

Dream boldly, dig deep in Scripture, and protect your foundation. Let's get started with building your house!

Chapter 4 *Reflection Questions*:

1. How would you describe your current
    foundation: both spiritually and relationally?
    In what ways is it aligned with God's design
    for your life?
2. What dreams or aspirations has God placed
    in your heart that you may have neglected,
    and what steps can you take to begin
    pursuing them intentionally?
3. Which areas of your marriage or personal life
    need clearer definitions, expectations,
    communication, or roles, to prevent
    misunderstandings and build trust?
4. How do the words you use to describe your
    ideal marriage reflect God's Word, and how
    can you actively live out those qualities in
    your relationship?
5. When faced with doubt, fear, or external
    negativity, how can you protect your
    God-given dreams and maintain a focus on
    hope, trust, and perseverance?

Part 2

BATHROOM

CHAPTER 5

The Bathroom Mirror - Facing Ourselves First

You can't live in a house without a bathroom. Not even for five hours. Especially if you have kids. It's essential. That's why, as we begin our journey through the metaphorical rooms of the home, we start in the bathroom. Because before we can address any relationship, especially marriage, we must first face ourselves.

The Place We Start and the Place We Hide

The bathroom is the first stop in our day. It's where we clean up, get ready, and prepare to present ourselves to the world. But it's also the first place we learn to cover up. From the earliest age, we're taught to mask our imperfections, to make ourselves "presentable." We put on makeup, fix our hair, and choose the right clothes. In many ways, the bathroom is the room of transformation - but not always the kind that reflects the truth of who we are.

In our marriages, it's the same. When tension rises, the natural impulse is to point fingers. We blame. We deflect. But God calls us to something radically different: to first examine ourselves.

"Why do you look at the speck of sawdust in your
brother's eye and pay no attention to the plank in
your own eye?"
Matthew 7:3

Wearing the Mask

We all wear masks. Some physical. Most emotional.

The word "mask" is defined as something worn on
the face for protection, disguise, performance, or
entertainment. Ironically, these are the same
reasons we hide who we really are:

1. Protection

Masks keep us safe. Or at least, they feel like they
do. Behind them, we hide our pain, fears,
insecurities, and the lies we've believed - often from
childhood. Maybe a parent said you'd never amount
to anything. Maybe a partner made you feel
unlovable. Sometimes, the very person we share a
home with makes us feel we have to stay hidden just
to survive emotionally.

2. Disguise

Think about the costume you wear each day. Are
you the mom who "has it all together"? The dad who
walks into work with confidence but is falling apart
inside? The churchgoer who knows all the right
words, yet dreads going home? We disguise our
truth to appear composed, capable, or strong. But at
what cost?

3. Performance

Many of us have been acting for years. We play the part others expect: the responsible one, the nurturing one, the successful one. You might even know your "role" so well you forget who you are without the script.

4. Entertainment

Sometimes we participate just to be accepted. Join the club, volunteer for the event, attend the social gathering. Not because we want to, but because we hope it will make us feel like we belong. We become who others want us to be, not who God designed us to be.

Why We Wear Masks

Here are four key influences that drive us to live behind emotional masks:

Social Media

No one posts their worst moments online. We scroll through a sea of filtered perfection and wonder why we don't measure up. But it's all a lie. One woman I knew posted smiling beach photos with her kids, and four hours later attempted suicide. Her online life was a façade hiding immense pain. We compare ourselves to illusions and slowly believe we are not enough.

Societal Expectations

Success, beauty, and achievement. Our culture defines what is valuable, and we chase it. As a result, we bend ourselves to fit the mold, even when it breaks us.

Social Circles

Even our friendships and community groups can pressure us to pretend. We avoid honesty out of fear we'll be judged or rejected. So, we silently suffer while keeping up appearances.

Family Pressures

For many, family roles run deep. Maybe your family still sees you as "the quiet one" or "the problem-solver" or "the one who can't handle things." We carry these labels into adulthood and conform to who we were, not who we've become, or who we want to be.

The Call to Authenticity

Jesus doesn't ask us to perform. He invites us to come as we are: broken, messy, real. When we face ourselves in the "bathroom mirror," we begin to see the parts of us that need grace, healing, and truth. Not to shame ourselves, but to start the transformation God truly desires for us.

True change in marriage, or any relationship, doesn't begin with fixing the other person. It begins in the mirror.

"Search me, God, and know my heart; test me and know my anxious thoughts." Psalm 139:23

The Mask in the Mirror

I still remember sitting at the dinner table growing up, flanked by two very outspoken siblings. They had big voices and strong opinions, loud presences that often filled the room. In contrast, I tended to shrink back, choosing silence over conflict. Not because I didn't have thoughts or feelings, but because I didn't want to compete with the stronger personalities. It's funny how those old family roles can follow us into adulthood. I've grown a lot since then. In most areas of life now, I speak up. I share my thoughts, lead conversations, and contribute with confidence. But every now and then, especially when I'm around my family of origin, I feel myself shrinking again. I walk into a room and instinctively fall back into that quiet role, like an old coat that no longer fits but still hangs in the closet.

Why do we do that? Why do we revert? And more importantly, why do we keep hiding behind masks, even when we know it's not our true self?

We all do it. In our families, in our churches, at our jobs. It's the performance. The projection. The carefully curated version of ourselves we offer to the world.

The Checklist Christian

Take church, for example. How easy it is to start measuring our faith by someone else's schedule. *How many Bible studies is she doing? Is she in BSF? Oh wow, she's volunteering too?* Suddenly, faith becomes a checklist. It's not enough to *believe*. We feel the pressure to *prove* our belief through action and achievement. And if we're honest, sometimes it's less about glorifying God and more about looking like the "perfect Christian woman."

But God never asked us to perform. He asked us to be faithful.

The Workplace Mask

At work, we wear the "I've got it all together" mask. Even on the hardest days, we walk into the office with a forced smile and a steady voice. That's not always wrong! There's wisdom in professionalism. But somewhere along the line, many of us decided vulnerability has no place in the workplace.

And yet, it's often in those authentic moments that trust is born. That man in the next cubicle might be carrying his own silent burden. Your honesty could be the bridge that connects his pain to hope. But we miss those moments when we stay hidden.

We perform. Constantly. The effort we pour into looking like we have it together could win us an Oscar.

I sat with a couple whose lives were falling apart in private. Hours later, I watched them at a church event with their arms around each other, smiling as though nothing was wrong. The gap between their real selves and their presented selves was painful to witness.

What is it that keeps us from being real?

The Mask Exercise

When working with couples, my husband and I have passed out paper masks and given them this simple assignment:

On the front of your mask, write down words that describe how you present yourself when you leave your house.

You don't have to go deep, just be honest. Maybe you write *confident, happy, successful.* Or maybe it's *busy, put together, fine.*

None of these are wrong. Sometimes we really *are* confident. But sometimes we're just really good at pretending.

Then, we have discussed: *Which influence is most responsible for you wearing that mask?*

- Social media?
- Friends and family?
- Cultural expectations?
- Faith performance?
- Work persona?
- The pressure to appear perfect?

Take a moment and ask yourself: What mask do I wear most often? And why?

Broken to Be Built

I watched a great video of Marine recruits arriving at boot camp. They were wide-eyed, nervous, and standing tall in brand-new uniforms. Within seconds, the drill instructor was in their faces, shouting commands. It was intense. Jarring.

Why so harsh?

Because those young recruits are being prepared for the front lines. Boot camp isn't about punishment, it's about preparation. To survive, they must be broken down and rebuilt. Every weakness exposed. Every illusion stripped away. Because in battle, the cost of not knowing your limits is life and death.

And then I thought - *isn't God a bit like that too?*

He's not some whispering voice gently asking you to "consider growth when you're comfortable." He's a Commander calling you into battle. He wants you to know who you *really* are, not just for your sake, but for the sake of those around you.

We are in a war every day, against lies, against shame, against the enemy of our souls. If we don't know who we are, we will fall.

Facing the Mirror

God is not casual about this. He commands us to examine ourselves, to look in the mirror and ask:

- Who am I becoming?
- Who has He called me to be?
- What am I hiding behind?

And more importantly:

- *Do I believe the lies Satan tells me about who I am?*
- *Am I allowing those lies to shape my thoughts, emotions, and reactions?*

If you don't face the truth of what's going on inside of you, those lies will become weapons; not just against yourself, but against your spouse, your children, your friends.

We cannot afford to take this lightly.

The Courage to Look Inward

There came a time in my life and marriage where I had to stop blaming others. I had to pause and look in the mirror. Not to condemn myself, but to *own my part*, to understand what patterns I carried, what triggers I hadn't healed, what emotional walls I had built.

I did something terrifying. I sat down with the people who knew me best: my sister, my brother, my parents, my closest friends. I asked them to tell me the truth about me.

"What do you see in me that I'm not seeing? What are my blind spots? My strengths? My weaknesses? The patterns I'm repeating?"

It was humbling. Vulnerable. Painful.

But it was also healing.

Because I discovered two important truths:

1. The things I thought I was hiding were more visible than I realized.
2. I was stronger than I believed.

I had underestimated both my brokenness and my resilience.

A Three-Step Battle Plan

So, what can you do?

Here's a three-step process to start living unmasked:

1. **Know Yourself**
   What fears, insecurities, or past wounds cause you to react instead of respond? Take assessments to learn more about why you react the way you do. (Some great assessments include The Enneagram, DISC, Strength Finders, and Attachment Style). The more you understand yourself, the good and the bad, the more you will be able to know

what to work on and how to define what you
need.

2. **Decide to Dig Deep**
   Are you willing to fight for the people you
   love by first fighting to know yourself?

3. **Respond, Don't React**
   Scripture calls us to respond with wisdom,
   not to react out of emotion. Reactions come
   from wounds. Responses come from healing.

Reminder

God is not looking for your perfection. He's calling
for your **authenticity**.

You have a choice every single day:

Will you live from the identity He gave you or the
image you think the world wants to see?

Take off the mask. Look in the mirror. Start
becoming who you already are in Christ.

Chapter 5 *Reflection Questions:*

1. What emotional or social "masks" do I find myself wearing most often, and what influences (social media, family, work, or cultural expectations) encourage me to wear them?
2. When I look in the metaphorical bathroom mirror, what aspects of myself am I avoiding, hiding, or afraid to confront?
3. How have my past experiences, triggers, or family roles shaped the way I present myself to others, and how might they be impacting my marriage or relationships today?
4. In what areas of my life am I responding out of fear, insecurity, or performance instead of acting from authenticity, faith, and self-awareness?
5. What steps can I take to face my blind spots, embrace my true self, and respond to challenges with wisdom and grace rather than reacting from emotional wounds?

CHAPTER 6

Behind the Mask: The Power of Choice

We don't always get to control what we feel, but we do get to choose what we do next.

Have you ever found yourself thinking, *I don't want to feel this way*? That overwhelming surge of emotion that seems to grip you without your consent – frustration, anger, anxiety. It shows up uninvited. But here's the truth: we have a choice. Even in those moments, we can decide to take control before our emotions take over.

It starts with this: *I'm not going to allow this battle of emotions to overtake me.*

Choosing to stop yourself: to take a deep breath, to pause before reacting! This is one of the most powerful spiritual muscles we can develop. Even when your emotions haven't caught up, your responses still can.

Let's say you're angry. Really angry. Your child or spouse has pushed every single button you didn't even know you had. You might feel like screaming. But even then, you can choose: *I'm not going to say what I'm feeling until I calm down.*

Sometimes that choice looks as simple as walking around the block or clenching your mouth shut, quite literally, if needed, just to avoid saying something you'll regret five minutes later.

This is the daily invitation of maturity: emotional, relational, and spiritual maturity. It's the practice of choosing thought, emotion, and response *on purpose*.

Training Your Reactions

This isn't easy. It's not even natural. But it is *possible* and transformational.

I see it every day with my kids. They know how to press me, and I often want to react in frustration. But the moment I stop and take a deep breath, just five seconds, I give myself space to choose a better way.

Try this: next time you feel the surge rising, pause. Breathe. And think to yourself:

Thought → Emotion → Reaction or Response

This is incredibly important. More important than most of us realize.

When we react to something, it feels instant. Someone says something, and boom - we snap back, shut down, or walk away stewing. But what we often don't recognize is that our reaction is actually the *third* step in a mental and emotional process. There's a progression that happens, and it's fast, automatic, and powerful. The key to responding instead of reacting is learning to slow that process down.

Let's break it down.

Step 1: The Thought

Every reaction begins with a thought. Maybe someone makes a comment, or something unexpected happens. Imagine you arrive late to a gathering, and a friend jokingly says, "Big surprise, they're not on time."

You laugh on the outside, but inside your mind is racing:

"They don't think I'm reliable."
"What else do they say about me behind my back?"
"They don't know that my life is overwhelming right now and it's a miracle I even showed up."

In the blink of an eye, your brain fills with messages; some based in truth, others shaped by insecurity, stress, or past experiences.

Step 2: The Feeling

Next comes the emotional response. You might feel angry, unseen, frustrated, or even shamed. And here's what's so easy to miss: those feelings didn't come out of nowhere. They're a direct result of the thoughts you had.

But it happens fast, so fast that we often skip this awareness altogether and we move straight to step three.

Step 3: The Reaction

This is when we respond outwardly. Maybe it's with a passive-aggressive jab like, "Well, if I only had one child instead of three, I'd be on time too." Maybe you just roll your eyes, or maybe you decide silently: *I'm not talking to her for the rest of the day.*

These reactions often come from a place of self-protection. They're usually quick, defensive, and harsh and often escalate the situation rather than resolving anything.

The Shift: From Reaction to Response

So how do we change this pattern?

The goal isn't to eliminate emotions or avoid difficult moments. The goal is to *respond* rather than react. And to do that, we must slow down the 3-step process.

Start with the Thought

When a comment triggers you, and your mind starts spiraling, stop. Pause and ask: *What's really true?* You have the power to change the narrative in your head.

Instead of:
"They don't respect me."
Try:
"They don't know that I was waiting on the refrigerator repair person this morning."
Or:
"It's actually amazing I made it here with three kids in tow."
Or even:
"A late arrival to a relaxed playdate doesn't define my value."

And most importantly:
"God sees me. He loves me. And He is not measuring my worth by punctuality."

Truth-centered thoughts create space for grace. Both for yourself and for others.

Calm the Emotion

Let's say the thoughts are still swirling. That's okay. You still have a choice. You can stop and calm your body before the emotions take over.

1. Inhale slowly through your nose for a count of 4 seconds
2. Hold your breath for a count of 7
3. Exhale for a count of 8
4. Repeat this cycle for 3-4 rounds

This simple rhythm helps regulate your nervous system. Once your body is calm, you'll often find

that you no longer feel the urgent need to react.
What once felt big begins to shrink.

The Practice of Choosing a Response

Here's the truth: **You are not powerless.** You
control your responses. You get to decide whether to
react or to respond. But it takes practice.

Start small. Notice the moments during your day
when you're triggered. Pause. Breathe. Choose a
new thought. Diffuse the feeling.

The more you practice slowing down this process,
the more natural it becomes. And then, when the
big things come, and they *will* come, you'll have the
tools to respond with grace and confidence.

* Just remember, be aware that there are
controllable factors that can help you to learn to
respond ... eat food that gives you energy (and you
aren't hangry and expect to make a good decision),
get enough sleep, have a good friend to call who can
"talk you off the ledge", and take a walk around the
block if needed! *

Choosing Armor Over Appearance

There's a deeper shift that we're invited into, one
that goes beyond emotional self-control. It's about
what we choose to put on every day.

And it's not just our clothes, our makeup, or the
image we present to the world.

Instead of putting on your mask every single day, put on the **armor of God**.

Let's read this together, slowly and intentionally, from Ephesians 6:10–17:

"Finally, be strong in the Lord and in the strength of His might. Put on the whole armor of God, that you may be able to stand against the schemes of the devil. For we do not wrestle against flesh and blood, but against the rulers, against the authorities, against the cosmic powers over this present darkness, against the spiritual forces of evil in the heavenly places. Therefore take up the whole armor of God, that you may be able to withstand in the evil day, and having done all, to stand firm. Stand therefore, having fastened on the belt of truth, and having put on the breastplate of righteousness, and, as shoes for your feet, having put on the readiness given by the gospel of peace.
In all circumstances take up the shield of faith, with which you can extinguish all the flaming darts of the evil one; and take the helmet of salvation, and the sword of the Spirit, which is the word of God."

This is the armor we need. Not just for surviving the day, but for becoming who God has called us to be.

Train for the Battle You Can't See

Let's stop pretending that life isn't a spiritual battlefield.

We are not each other's enemies, though we often live that way. Our true enemy is Satan. And he is clever. He works through our distractions, our bitterness, our pride, and our unhealed places. He works through our *masks*.

So take up your armor. Train. Don't coast through marriage. Don't just react to the changes in your life. Prepare for them.

Twice a year, my husband and I set aside time for evaluation. To ask each other hard questions, to assess where we are, and to make adjustments. Why? Because life keeps changing. Kids grow. Work changes. Health changes. *We* change. (This planning session will be covered in detail in the "Kitchen" chapter.)

Training doesn't end once you say "I do." It's a lifelong journey of preparation and growth;so that when the hard moments come, you're *ready*.

Faith, Focus, and the Word

Remember who God is. He is Immanuel, meaning "God with us."

He is *with you*. He is sitting beside you right now. He is not distant or disinterested. He is your Father, your Comforter, your Warrior, your Savior.

So let Him be your *compass*.
Let Scripture be the guide you return to every single day.

We invest time in our masks daily. What would change if we invested the same effort in putting on our spiritual armor?

Because the truth is: this battle is *real*. And it's already happening.

To know yourself, really know yourself, you must look into the Word. You must let it reflect back to you the places where you still need healing, where you're not yet who God is calling you to be.

That's where transformation begins.

Coming Clean: A New Kind of Bathroom Talk

And now, let's talk about the other thing that happens in the bathroom.

I know, not glamorous. But hear me out.

Every human body needs to eliminate waste. When we don't, it builds up, makes us sick, and eventually incapacitates us.

It's the same spiritually and emotionally. We need to regularly deal with the *toxic stuff* inside us: old pain, shame, bitterness, trauma. If we don't, it starts to poison our thoughts, our marriage, our parenting, and our faith.

It *must* come out.

But here's the thing: **it's a process**. *You can't just snap your fingers and get rid of years of buildup. It starts with awareness. It continues with grace. It ends in freedom.*

So today, we begin that process. Together.

1. When you experience strong emotions, how often do you pause before reacting, and what might change if you practiced choosing your response more intentionally?

2. How do your automatic thoughts influence your emotions and reactions, and what truth-centered thoughts could help you respond with grace instead of reacting impulsively?

3. In what areas of your life are you still relying on masks rather than putting on the "armor of God," and what would it look like to replace performance with spiritual preparedness?

4. What toxic or unresolved emotions, past pains, or bitterness might you need to "come clean" about in order to experience emotional and spiritual freedom?

5. How can the practice of slowing down the Thought → Feeling → Reaction process transform your relationships and your personal spiritual growth?

CHAPTER 7

What's Making You Sick?

"You are what you eat." We've heard the phrase before, but what if it applies to more than just food? What if it touches the hidden parts of our lives; the patterns, addictions, wounds, and relationships we consume every day?

Movie Night... with a Message

Let me set the scene. It's movie night. Not your typical lighthearted comedy, but something with a bit more punch: **"Super Size Me."** It's a documentary from years back that follows a guy who eats nothing but McDonald's for 30 days straight. Breakfast, lunch, and dinner. Every item on the menu. Every time he's asked, "Would you like to supersize that?" he says yes.

No, this isn't a commentary on fast food or a campaign against McDonald's. The point is much deeper. As I watched this man's health decline over just 30 days, it made me think about how we live our lives and what we consume - not just our eating habits; our **emotional diet**, our **spiritual diet**, and our **relational diet**.

What are you regularly feeding your mind, your heart, your soul?

The Decay Begins Slowly

At first, the guy's laughing. He's loving his Egg McMuffin and Big Mac. It's familiar. It's fun. It's harmless.

Isn't that how most destructive habits start?

Maybe it's curiosity. Maybe it's stress relief. Maybe it just feels good. But almost without noticing, what begins as an indulgence quickly becomes a pattern. And patterns can become addictions.

By day three, the man eating only McDonald's is nauseous, exhausted, and shaky. But he pushes through;and his body adjusts. That's the danger: our minds and hearts can get used to things that are making us sick. Emotional toxins can settle in like old furniture - we hardly notice them anymore.

He begins waking up with chest pain. Walking up stairs becomes difficult. He's depressed. He's anxious. And yet, he keeps eating. Because by now, he's hooked.

This is a metaphor for our lives.

What Are You Feeding Your Life?

If we're honest, most of us are consuming something that's hurting us. Not always food; sometimes it's **media**, sometimes it's **comparison**, sometimes it's **shame**. These toxins accumulate, and unless we recognize them and stop the cycle, they will destroy us.

By the end of the movie, his body is breaking down. His liver is sick. His cholesterol is off the charts. His emotional state is unrecognizable. All of this - just from feeding himself the wrong things consistently.

The big question isn't "Why did he eat McDonald's?"

The big question is **"What are YOU feeding yourself that's slowly killing you?"**

Step One: Recognize What Is Making You Sick

You can't fix what you won't face. Before we talk about healing, we need to talk about **toxic intake**; the things you've absorbed into your life, mind, and spirit that are making you sick.

Addictions

Addictions can start small; seemingly harmless. But over time, they twist themselves into our lives. Whether you've experienced these firsthand or walked with someone who has, the effects are the same: the addictions promise short term relief but deliver bondage.

Addictions can include:

- Pornography
- Alcohol or drugs
- Shopping (yes, really;especially if it's used to numb pain or gain identity)
- Gambling

- Technology: phones, games, screens, social media
- Food: a gift from God, but a dangerous idol if misused
- Smoking
- Work: especially when driven by approval, perfectionism, or fear
- Gossip: using drama to distract from your own brokenness
- Attention: being an "attention junkie" can hide deep insecurities

Addictions change the way you think, feel, and interact. They reshape your brain, your relationships, your time, your focus;and ultimately your future. They may not all physically kill you, but they can destroy your **joy**, your **peace**, your **purpose**, and your **relationships**.

Step Two: Clean House

Imagine locking all the doors of your house at night, checking the windows, walking the perimeter. You're protecting your home. But how many of us protect **our internal home**;our minds, hearts, and spirits?

We wear seatbelts when in the car. We install security systems around our homes. But the real danger might not be outside.

The real danger might be the hidden habits, beliefs, or wounds we've refused to deal with.

Emotional Abuse and Wounds

Are you carrying around pain you didn't choose? Emotional wounds, past abuse, and hurtful relationships leave marks that don't show on the outside, but they rot your foundations from within. Whether it's verbal, emotional, physical, or sexual abuse, these wounds must be faced with compassion, truth, and help.

Insecurity and Self-Image

How do you view yourself? What story plays in your mind about who you are;your worth, your value, your talents? If your inner voice constantly beats you down, it's hard to be present for the people who need you. If you're dying inside, it's nearly impossible to live well on the outside.

Unhealthy Relationships

Broken relationships leave more than just heartbreak. They can distort your view of love, trust, and even God. Maybe an old dating relationship left you insecure. Maybe your parents' dysfunction became your normal. Maybe a past friend betrayed you, and now you don't allow anyone to get too close.

Sometimes we carry **patterns** from past relationships. We compare our spouse to an ex. We replay old wounds in new settings. Even good past relationships can leave behind expectations that set us up for disappointment.

Step Three: Tell the Truth and Take the Steps

Healing starts with honesty. You have to be brave enough to look in the mirror and ask:

"What is making me sick inside?"
"What have I allowed into my life that is slowly destroying me?"

Then, with God's help and the support of trusted people, take action.

- **Tell someone.** Isolation fuels addiction and shame.
- **Get help.** Counseling, groups, accountability ;whatever it takes.
- **Start replacing lies with truth.** Saturate your mind with God's Word, not toxic self-talk.
- **Fight with faith.** The battle is spiritual. And you are not alone.

REMEMBER ....

You were created for freedom, not bondage. For joy, not despair. For wholeness, not sickness.

So let me ask you:
What are you feeding your soul?
What waste needs to be removed from your life?
What hidden habits are making you sick?

Jesus came to set the captives free. But we must step forward and unlock the chains. Today can be the time you start the process.

You lock your doors at night. Now, start guarding your heart.

Clearing the Waste – Breaking Free from Toxic Patterns

There's a certain kind of pain that comes not from something sudden or traumatic, but from patterns we've grown used to;habits of self-protection we built to survive. Maybe you moved around a lot as a child. Maybe people left. So you put up walls;just a little here and there. Nothing big. But enough to keep people from getting in. Because if they didn't get in, they couldn't hurt you.

You didn't even realize how much those walls shaped your adulthood. I didn't.

Then there are those deep-rooted patterns ...

When my husband and I got married, we each brought our patterns to the table. One example for our marriage was simply the differences in our resources growing up. Gregg grew up with very few resources. Not "we didn't have cable" poor. I mean "get clothes out of donation bags" poor. So, when he started a business and we began making money, he held on tightly to everything we had. He couldn't let go of old stuff, even if we didn't need it. Why? Because he figured maybe someday we *would* need it. And if we had to buy it again, that meant spending money;something he had been trained to fear.

It wasn't about the objects. It was about security. However, I came from a family who had a few more resources, and so if something was not working we could replace it. We moved a lot as well, so did not hold onto stuff that was not necessary. When I wanted to get rid of stuff once married, my husband pushed back. "We might need it!" he would argue. But it wasn't about the stuff;it was about our worlds colliding.

Two upbringings. Two stories. Two patterns.

Patterns that Collide

Then there were communication differences!

My family? Diplomatic, conversational, fast-paced. Each person almost always had something to say. Silence wasn't welcome;it meant the conversation had died.

Gregg's family? They functioned very differently. You let someone finish their thought, wait a beat, *then* maybe respond. That's just how it was.

So when we were dating in college, we had a night that nearly ended our relationship. We were walking and talking;or rather, I was talking. Nonstop. Gregg thought, *"She doesn't care what I have to say."* And I thought, *"He doesn't care enough to say anything."*

It wasn't true. We just had completely different communication patterns. I thought silence was rejection. He thought talking without pausing meant domination.

We both felt unloved. Misunderstood.

And we almost broke up.

Only later did we realize the disconnect wasn't about love;it was about wiring. And that wiring came from our pasts.

When the Past Sneaks In

Not everything we bring into our relationships is toxic in and of itself. Sometimes it's good;until it's not. Patterns from childhood, ways of coping, learned roles, or emotional reflexes;they can be deeply ingrained and hard to see clearly.

You might have communication breakdowns in your marriage. Or conflict with your kids. And you might not even realize it stems from old wiring;wounds or routines you never flushed out.

Ask yourself:

- What shaped your responses, beliefs, and behaviors?
- Are you aware of the patterns you've inherited or developed?
- Are they affecting your spouse, children, or relationships?

These things; our histories, addictions, wounds;they don't just sit quietly in a corner. They influence our moods, our time, our reactions. And if left unchecked, they begin to **consume** us.

Flush It Out

Have you ever truly flushed those things out?

It's a hard question, but a necessary one:

Maybe you've been avoiding something painful for years. Maybe you never realized something even needed flushing. But the truth is, when left inside, unspoken and unhealed, it *stinks*. And that stink? It builds walls.

Walls to hide the odor.
Walls to keep people out.
Walls that isolate and harden.

Eventually, even the people who love you most start pulling away. Not because they don't care;but because something in you pushes them back.

We have to recognize the stink and flush it out. That might mean revisiting old pain. It might mean uncovering deeply rooted patterns. But it also might mean finally taking back ground the enemy has claimed in your life.

What Scripture Says

This battle of the mind and flesh? It's not new. Scripture gives us a map for how to navigate it:

Galatians 6:7–9 – "Do not be deceived: God cannot be mocked. A man reaps what he sows.

Whoever sows to please their flesh, from the flesh will reap destruction..."

2 Corinthians 10:3–5 – "...the weapons we fight with are not the weapons of the world...they have divine power to demolish strongholds."

Romans 7:21–25 – "Although I want to do good, evil is right there with me...What a wretched man I am! Who will rescue me? Thanks be to God;who delivers me through Jesus Christ our Lord!"

Romans 8:5–6 – "The mind governed by the flesh is death, but the mind governed by the Spirit is life and peace."

These aren't just abstract verses. They're weapons. They're anchors. And they remind us of truth:

There's no shame in needing help. Admitting you need help starts the process of healing. It's time. Today.

What if your pattern involves addiction? Or insecurity? What if you're dealing with pornography, substance abuse, financial recklessness, or deep emotional wounding?

Owning it won't be easy. In fact, it might cost you something. It may lead to difficult conversations, painful admissions, or consequences you've been dreading.

But what's the alternative?

Letting it fester? Letting it rot everything good in your life?

We've got to be brave enough to say, *"I'm broken."* Brave enough to step into the light. Brave enough to invite healing; even if it hurts at first.

Because here's the truth: healing *is* painful. But *not healing* is deadly.

Living According to the Word

If we want freedom - real, lasting freedom;we have to root ourselves in Scripture. Psalm 119 gives us a clear answer:

Psalm 119:9–10 – "How can a young person stay on the path of purity? By living according to your word. I seek you with all my heart; do not let me stray from your commands."

It's not complicated. But it *is* hard.

We pursue purity and healing by living according to God's Word. Spending time in Scripture. Listening for His voice. Seeking His heart.

This is our lifeline.
This is how we keep our way pure.
This is how we flush out what's toxic.

The Invitation

You're not alone in your struggle. Every single one of us is in a battle. Between the Spirit and the flesh. Between old patterns and new life. Between pride and humility. Between bondage and freedom.

But freedom is possible.

And it begins when we get honest.
It begins when we flush the waste.
It begins when we let God transform our minds;and renew our hearts.

Take the step. Ask for help. Return to the Word.
 And let the healing begin.

There comes a point in every person's journey when we must whisper;or cry out;those honest, humbling words: *I need help.*

That moment of surrender is often the first step toward real healing. It's where the transformation begins;not just in our relationships, but deep within our own hearts. Some of us are carrying pain, habits, or hidden battles that have lived inside us for years;since childhood even. They've shaped our decisions, our patterns, and the way we relate to others.

But God offers us something better.

Yes, the process of healing is hard. It's scary. It's embarrassing. It may even carry real consequences. But in taking that first step and asking for help, we begin to move from death into life. We start a new journey; one marked by freedom, purpose, and spiritual renewal. And that is a beautiful, holy gift.

Chapter 7 *Reflection Questions*:

1. What are the emotional, spiritual, or relational "foods" you are regularly consuming, and how might they be impacting your overall well-being?
2. Which hidden patterns, addictions, or unresolved wounds in your life have you become accustomed to, even if they are slowly harming you?
3. How have past experiences, family dynamics, or childhood patterns shaped the way you think, respond, and relate to others today?
4. In what areas of your life might you need to take honest steps to "flush out" toxic habits, beliefs, or relationships, and what practical actions could help you start that process?
5. How can grounding yourself in God's Word and seeking support from trusted people guide you toward freedom, healing, and transformation in your mind, heart, and relationships?

CHAPTER 8

You Are Not Alone

Let's be clear: you cannot conquer these things on your own. I know I couldn't. But the good news is, you're not expected to.

Scripture tells us we have *divine power* at work within us
(2 Corinthians 10:4). We have God on our side;doing things in and around us that we could never accomplish on our own. That's not just poetic language. It's the truth. God steps into our mess with power that can transform us from the inside out.

So how do we begin?

Step One: Invite the Holy Spirit

The first and most important place to start is with God Himself. Talk to Him. Pray. Bring your honest heart before Him.

When I was in the middle of my own chaos, I had no idea what to do. But I began to pray;raw, honest prayers like, "Lord, I don't know how to fix this. I don't know how to stop what's happening inside me. I can't do it anymore."

And something shifted.

I let go of control. I stopped trying to fix myself and gave it over to God. That surrender; painful and vulnerable - was the beginning of real change.

Because only in brokenness can we be rebuilt by the hand of the Healer.

Will it hurt? Yes. But you can trust God with that pain. He will lead you through it. And over time, He'll take your mess and turn it into something beautiful.

Step Two: Seek Out Wisdom

Start with the Word. Scripture is not just an old book;it's a living, breathing source of counsel and truth. Every time you open it, it has something new to say. It speaks to exactly what we need in each moment. As it says in Hebrew 4:12: "For the word of God is alive and active. Sharper than any double-edged sword."

Also be willing to reach out for practical help. I went to counseling. And honestly? It wasn't glamorous. I sat there and "vomited" words; just talked and talked and got it all out. And somewhere in the middle of it, I started to hear myself clearly. I started to realize, *Oh, that's what's really going on.*

Sometimes, hearing your own voice speak the truth aloud is what breaks denial and begins the healing.

But here's the key: be humble enough to listen. Don't just vent - learn. Take advice. Let others speak into your blind spots. I'll admit: for me, that's hard. I hate being told what to do. But real growth requires us to lay down our pride and receive truth.

Step Three: Build Your Support Team

You don't need just a counselor. You need a whole team.

Find a mentor - someone who's a few steps ahead in life or faith. Someone who's been through the fire and come out refined. They don't need to be older, just wiser in certain areas.

Put accountability structures in place. Maybe that means a friend who checks in on you. Maybe it's installing a filter on your phone or canceling certain subscriptions. It might feel like a prison at first, but sometimes we need boundaries in order to breathe freely again.

And most importantly, surround yourself with community. We are not meant to do life alone.

Find friends who make you laugh, who walk with you through the hard stuff, and who love you enough to call you out when you're stuck in your own mess.

A Personal Example

Let me share an example from our own life. Gregg and I had a disagreement. We couldn't resolve it, and emotions ran high. One of my best friends, Jaime, happened to be visiting. She's known both of us for decades. She sat between us and said, "Okay, you give your side. Now you give yours." And then she looked at me and said, "You're being selfish," and turned to Gregg and said, "You need to grow up."

It was brutally honest. And exactly what we needed. Because we had given her permission to speak into our lives like that.

That kind of truth-telling friendship is a *gift*.

If you don't have that, seek it out. Be intentional. Define what you need and ask others to walk that road with you. When Gregg and I lived in Virginia, I had an accountability group of five women who I shared life with; we called it "lay-it-on-the-table accountability." No secrets. Just the truth. And it changed us.

Scripture for the Journey

Let God's Word guide you. Let it convict and comfort you.

"The way of a fool is right in his own eyes, but a wise man listens to advice."
 - Proverbs 12:15

"Without counsel plans fail, but with many advisers they succeed."
 - Proverbs 15:22

"Listen to advice and accept instruction, that you may gain wisdom in the future."
 - Proverbs 19:20

"When pride comes, then comes disgrace, but with humility comes wisdom."
 - Proverbs 11:2

How often do we ignore what God has already laid out for us? He's given us the blueprint. We just need to follow it.

The Power of Light

There is *freedom* in letting go.

Go back to that feeling of being physically ill;your chest heaving, your body aching. That's what emotional and spiritual darkness feels like inside us. But when we bring it into the light;when we confess it to God and to others. It loses its grip.

Yes, the journey is hard. Yes, it's life-altering. But it's also life-giving.

When we bring darkness into the light, it cannot stay. It has no power. And we step into the truth of who God is.

"Thanks be to God that, though you used to be slaves to sin, you have come to obey from your heart... You have been set free from sin and have become slaves to righteousness."
 - Romans 6:17–18

"Now, by dying to what once bound us, we have been released... so that we serve in the new way of the Spirit."
 - Romans 7:6

That's how real change happens;not by willpower, but by surrendering to the Spirit of God. It's the only way we can truly be made new.

"This is the message we have heard from Him and declare to you: God is light; in Him there is no darkness at all."
 - 1 John 1:5

"So let us put aside the deeds of darkness and put on the armor of light - Romans 13:12

Take the Step

Ask for help.

Invite the Holy Spirit in.

Build a team.

Walk in the light.

Because freedom is possible, and it's more beautiful than you ever imagined.

Light in the House ; Clearing Space for the New

"God is light; in him there is no darkness at all. If we claim to have fellowship with him and yet walk in the darkness, we lie and do not live out the truth. But if we walk in the light, as he is in the light, we have fellowship with one another, and the blood of Jesus, his Son, purifies us from all sin."
 - 1 John 1:5–7

Renovation Starts with Light

Before you can renovate a house, you have to face what's in it. Turn on the lights. Open the closets. Pull back the rugs. God invites us to do the same with our hearts and our homes.

We often want to skip ahead to the exciting parts: redesigning communication, rebuilding trust, deepening intimacy. But the truth is, if the foundation isn't clean, anything new will eventually crack or collapse. This is why spiritual renovation begins with light;exposing what's hidden, toxic, or weighing us down.

So ask yourself: **Are you walking in the light? Or just playing pretend?**

We must pause here before going further. Because if we don't face our own brokenness, no new technique or strategy will truly stick. It's like trying to decorate a room infested with mold; eventually, it will eat through everything.

Real healing begins with **truth and transparency** - not just with each other, but with God. He already knows it all anyway. Walking in the light is not about perfection. It's about honesty.

"Search me, O God, and know my heart; test me and know my anxious thoughts." - Psalm 139:23

Toxic Clutter: Making Space for God's Best

We can't receive new life from God if our lives are cluttered with old wounds, sin patterns, or resentment. Those things don't just sit quietly in the corner; they sabotage progress, erode dreams, and plant fear.

Remember when I told you to write down your dreams? Those dreams are in danger if you don't clear the space for them to grow. Toxic emotions and unhealed patterns will attack those dreams like weeds in a garden.

So, I will ask again: **Are you willing to flush out what you need to? Are you willing to make room for the new?**

This is not just a spiritual ideal;it's a very practical step in your marriage. Until you clear the old pain and bitterness, there won't be space for laughter, closeness, or dreams fulfilled.

Grace for the Journey

This kind of honesty can be heavy. It's hard work. But that's why grace matters so much.

Give each other space. Give each other gentleness. Some of you may be ready to dive deep; others may still be cautiously standing at the edge. That's okay.

If you are carrying more visible wounds than your spouse, give yourself grace. Don't rush the process and don't feel shame!

Offer each other support. Offer each other grace. We all need healing. We all need God.

And when you do talk;whether with your spouse or a trusted friend;cover those conversations in **prayer, patience, and love**. Accountability doesn't have to sound like criticism. It can sound like encouragement: *"Let's not go backward. Let's move forward;together."*

Resources for When It Gets Hard

I know some of this content touches deep wounds;things like addiction, past trauma, or deep patterns of dysfunction. You don't have to walk through those alone.

Reach out to your local church, or to a counseling center and find groups or counselors that can walk this road with you!

Don't hesitate to reach out. Sometimes the bravest step you can take is the one that says: *"I need help."*

A Final Encouragement

God doesn't expose the dark to shame you. He does it to **heal you**. To bring light. To bring life. He loves you too much to leave you in hiding.

This chapter isn't about blame; it's about invitation. To step into the light. To clear out the old. To make space for God to do something new and beautiful in your life, your marriage, and your home.

Chapter 8 *Reflection Questions*:

1. In what areas of your life are you trying to manage or fix things on your own, and how might inviting the Holy Spirit in change your approach?
2. How open are you to seeking wisdom from Scripture, mentors, or counselors, and what might be keeping you from fully listening and receiving guidance?
3. Who makes up your support team, and are there relationships or accountability structures you need to build to walk in truth and growth?
4. What "darkness" or hidden struggles in your heart and life need to be brought into the light for healing and transformation to occur?
5. How willing are you to clear out old wounds, toxic patterns, or resentment to make space for God's new work in your life and relationships?

Part 3

MASTER BEDROOM

CHAPTER 9

Intimacy Begins with Communication

A Room Reserved for Intimacy

Welcome to the master bedroom; perhaps the most anticipated room in the metaphorical house of marriage. At first mention, many people jump straight to sex. And yes, sex is a part of it - but in this section, I'm unpacking a fuller definition of intimacy. The master bedroom represents something more sacred, more expansive. It's the space where a husband and wife share their most vulnerable, authentic selves. It's a room of connection;physically, emotionally, spiritually, and relationally.

In other words, it's not just about what happens under the covers. It's about what happens in the quiet moments of truth, the whispered conversations in the dark, the laughter after a long day, and the honest disagreements that stretch and shape you. It's about building trust in the most private parts of your marriage;physically, emotionally, and spiritually.

Tools for Renovation: A Night of Reflection and Realignment

I approach this chapter with humility. I'm not writing from a pedestal of perfection. I'm in this with you; learning, growing, sometimes stumbling, and getting back up again. This chapter isn't a formula or a fix-all. It's a toolbox, a set of practical and emotional resources to help you start conversations that matter.

Intimacy can be tough. It often brings with it wounds from the past, cultural confusion, or personal insecurities. But in this chapter, I want to create a safe space to talk about all of it;communication, friendship, sexuality, and spirituality;because you can't renovate what you refuse to acknowledge.

A Look Back: 1999 and a Wedding Band

Let me take you back to the golden days of the 1990s; a simpler, neon-colored time of mixtapes and cargo pants. For me, the '90s weren't just nostalgic; they were life-defining. I survived middle school, enjoyed high school, explored the world, met the love of my life, and got married in 1999. It was a great way to end the decade.

Back then, marriage felt like an exciting leap. I was in love. I was full of dreams. I was ready to party like it was 1999 (thanks, Prince). But marriage quickly revealed some hard truths: we were different. We had different pasts, different expectations, and different communication styles. Our desires and our emotional languages often clashed.

What I thought would be naturally easy - intimacy, communication, sex - wasn't. And like many young couples, we made the mistake of assuming things would "just get better" over time. But they didn't. In fact, our inability to talk honestly and openly became the very thing that unraveled us.

Seven years in, we hit a wall. Our lack of communication led to deep disconnection. We had built a marriage but neglected to furnish the master bedroom with the tools of understanding and vulnerability.

Why We Must Talk About Sex - and Everything Else

There's a 1991 classic by Salt-N-Pepa (yes, really) that says it well:

"Let's talk about sex, baby. Let's talk about you and me. Let's talk about all the good things and the bad things that may be..."

They weren't just singing;they were preaching. The reality is, sex is part of marriage, and it's deeply intertwined with how we communicate, how we feel safe, and how we understand each other. And yet, many couples avoid the topic altogether.

The lyrics go on to challenge us not to be coy or avoid the conversation because silence doesn't make the need go away. Avoidance often magnifies misunderstanding. That's why we're not just talking about sex in this chapter;we're talking about how to *talk* about sex. And even more foundationally, how to communicate in the vulnerable spaces that marriage invites us into.

Before the Bedroom: Communication is the Foundation

Before we can have honest conversations about physical intimacy, we have to learn how to talk;really talk. That starts with some foundational principles.

I realize this may feel like a buzzkill. But the truth is, great intimacy is built on great communication. And that starts with learning how to talk *before* you touch.

So let's start there;with a few communication "ground rules" that can strengthen every room in your relational house:

Communication Ground Rules

1. **Assume the Best** – Your spouse is not your enemy. Begin every hard conversation by reminding yourself, "This person loves me."
2. **Use "I" Statements** – Speak from your experience, not accusations. Instead of "You never listen," try "I feel unseen when I share and don't get a response."
3. **Pause, Don't Pounce** – If emotions are running high, take a break. Timeouts aren't avoidance;they're wisdom.
4. **Listen to Understand, Not to Win** – Sometimes your spouse doesn't need a solution;they just need to be heard.

5. **Create a Safe Zone** – Designate time and space to talk about difficult topics without distractions or interruptions.

The Hidden Layers of Intimacy

For some couples, physical intimacy comes easily, but conversation is a landmine. For others, communication flows, but there's a drought in the bedroom. Still others face deep wounds; past abuse, betrayal, shame that complicate connection in either area.

Let me say this: **you are not alone**.

Among the readers of this book - I know the stories are varied:

- Some of you feel like roommates instead of lovers.
- Some of you ache from unspoken needs.
- Some of you feel abandoned in your marriage bed.
- Others feel burdened by expectations or past trauma.

I want to honor that. And I want to say: don't stay silent. It's time to talk. To heal. To discover what intimacy can be;spiritually, emotionally, physically.

The Goal: Honest Connection Behind Closed Doors

The master bedroom is symbolic. It's the space where the rest of the world fades out, and just the two of you remain. And in that space, I believe deep healing and connection can happen. But it begins with learning to talk about the things we often hide.

So whether it's sex, finances, your in-laws, your fears, or your unmet needs; make the commitment to talk. This is your sacred space. Protect it. Nourish it. Be brave in it.

Because a healthy marriage isn't built on chemistry alone. It's built on communication, connection, and courage.

Communicating When It Counts

Conflict happens in every relationship. Whether you're coming through the door in a rage after a heated moment, or entering a seemingly simple conversation that suddenly unearths a mountain of unresolved emotion, communication becomes the bridge;or the battlefield. Regardless of how the conversation starts, how we handle it determines whether we build connection or deepen division.

This chapter is about biblical, grace-filled communication; especially in the heat of the moment. And let me be honest: my husband Gregg and I could not be more opposite when it comes to how we communicate. It's a miracle of God's grace that we've built a healthy, lasting marriage, because this part took serious work.

Opposites Do More Than Attract;They Clash

Gregg is a verbal processor. He knows what he wants, what he feels, and he's not shy to express it. I, on the other hand, am the classic middle child;peacemaker, agreeable, more inclined to say, "whatever you want" and tuck away my own feelings.

In our early marriage, this created an exhausting dynamic: he talked, and I shut down. He'd ask, "Aren't you angry?" I'd say, "Very." "About what?" "If you don't know, I'm not telling you."

What I didn't realize was how deeply unhealthy it was to suppress my feelings and expect Gregg to read my mind. I had to learn that my voice mattered;that communication wasn't just about being heard, but also about choosing to speak. Gregg had to learn to listen without pressuring. I had to learn to talk even when it was uncomfortable.

TOOLS

1. Be a Ready Listener

"Let every person be quick to hear, slow to speak, slow to anger..." James 1:19

This one sounds simple, but it's surprisingly hard;especially when emotions run high. Listening doesn't just mean staying quiet. It means being ready to listen. That takes intentionality. It means preparing your heart to truly hear, not just reload your next defense.

We did a little exercise in a class we taught: one person talked for two minutes about anything, and the other just listened;no comments, no nods, no corrections. At first, it felt awkward. But something amazing happened: people looked each other in the eye. They smiled. They felt heard. That's rare in daily life, especially in the middle of a conflict. Sometimes the most powerful way to honor your spouse is to simply stop and look them in the eye.

2. Be Slow to Speak

Sometimes we need a pause button. We call it the **10-second rule**: when you feel the heat rising, stop. Take a breath. Count to ten. Don't just fire back. Give your heart and brain a chance to align with the Spirit before your mouth jumps in.

If you're unsure of what your spouse meant, ask. Say, "Hey, I think I'm misunderstanding;are you saying ____?" Give them a chance to clarify. Don't assume. So much hurt comes from misinterpreted words.

And if you're the one being misunderstood, don't get defensive. Try again. Communication is about connection, not perfection.

3. Don't Let the Sun Go Down on Your Anger

"Do not let the sun go down while you are still
angry..."
 Ephesians 4:26

Every couple hears this verse. But let's be clear - it
doesn't mean you have to solve everything before
bed. It means don't let anger take root and fester.
Deal with the day's hurts before they harden into
bitterness.

Speak truth in love. And avoid exaggeration. "You
always..." "You never..." "You're just like your
mother..." Those phrases are verbal landmines.
They inflame and distort. Speak specifically. Speak
kindly. Speak truthfully.

4. Don't Use Silence as a Weapon

This one's personal for me. Silence was my go-to
defense. I knew it drove Gregg crazy when I shut
down, and in my pride, I used it to punish him.

But the truth is, silence - when it's used to hurt or
control - is just as damaging as yelling. So we made
a new rule: if I need time to process, I say so. I get
30 minutes. Then we come back and talk. Gregg
honors that time, and I commit to re-engage. It's no
longer a cold war tactic; it's a healthy pause with a
plan to reconnect.

5. Avoid Quarrels

You can disagree without quarreling. Quarreling is
disagreement wrapped in anger. It turns a

discussion into a win-lose battle. Remember: your spouse is not your enemy.

Learn to spot when your tone or body language crosses the line into combat mode. Step back. Breathe. Choose peace over pride.

6. Speak with Gentleness

"A gentle answer turns away wrath, but a harsh word stirs up anger." Proverbs 15:1

Even when you're hurt, even when you're right, gentleness is powerful. It doesn't mean weakness. It means strength under control. A kind tone softens hearts. Harsh words build walls. Don't confuse honesty with harshness. You can speak the truth with grace.

REMINDER

Communication isn't just a skill, it's a spiritual discipline. It's a daily opportunity to love like Christ, to listen like Jesus, to speak with wisdom, and to seek peace.

And don't forget - this isn't about perfection. Gregg and I are still learning, still failing, still trying again. But over time, God has taken our differences and turned them into something beautiful. And He can do the same for you.

So start small. Practice the ten-second pause. Talk about what each of your needs are in moments of conflict. And above all, invite God into the conversation. He is the best communicator of all.

1. How do you currently define intimacy in your marriage, and does it include emotional, spiritual, and relational connection as well as physical closeness?
2. In what ways do you practice;or avoid;honest communication with your spouse, especially about difficult topics or unmet needs?
3. Reflect on your communication patterns: Do you tend to speak from your feelings using "I" statements, or do you default to blame or silence? How might this impact intimacy?
4. How do you and your spouse handle conflict? Are there habits, like silence or defensiveness, that create distance instead of connection?
5. What practical steps can you take to create a "safe zone" for honest conversations and to invite God's guidance into your communication and intimacy?

CHAPTER 10

Communicating with Compassion:

Honoring Each Other in Conflict

Conflict is a natural part of any relationship. But how we handle it - especially in marriage - can either build trust or deeply erode it. Whether you're a shouter or someone who grows quiet in frustration, the key is not how conflict looks on the outside, but what's happening on the inside.

Uncontrolled anger can be incredibly destructive. Even if your version of anger doesn't involve raised voices, it still has an impact;on your heart, on your spouse, and especially on your children. We've worked with many couples over the years, and there have been moments - heartbreaking ones - when we've been on the phone with a couple who are yelling at each other while their kids are in the house, listening. They hear every word. They learn how to fight by watching you. And if their behavior mimicked yours at that moment, you'd be the first to correct them. So why do we allow ourselves to act that way toward our spouse?

Anger is not something to ignore or justify. If you or your spouse struggle with anger that feels out of control, please hear this clearly: be humble enough to get help. Uncontrolled anger can quickly cross into emotional, verbal, or even physical abuse. If you sense that line is being approached - or already crossed - reach out. Talk to a counselor or someone

you trust. Don't wait until more damage is done.
There is no shame in seeking help; in fact, it may be
one of the most courageous and loving decisions
you make.

*** If you are in a relationship where your spouse
abuses you emotionally, verbally, or physically -
TELL SOMEONE. Get help. It is NOT your fault
and is NEVER justified. This is also not something
you can fix by yourself. Reach out to a counselor or
a pastor and get yourself out of that situation until
your spouse is willing to get the help they need. ***

When You're Wrong;Admit It

It sounds simple, but it's one of the hardest things
in communication: when you're wrong, admit it.
Not with a "but" attached. Not with a justification or
excuse. Just acknowledge it.

"I was wrong. I see how that hurt you. I'm sorry."

Those words are powerful. But if we follow them
with a "but...";as in "I'm sorry, but you made me
mad," or "I didn't mean to, but you were being
dramatic";we undo the apology. For many years,
"but" played a starring role in our arguments. Gregg
(with his permission to share) would often say, "I'm
sorry, but..." and I'd immediately shut down.
Because what I heard was: "I'm not really sorry."
When we attach justifications, we remove the
weight of the apology.

And remember, even if you didn't *mean* to hurt your
spouse, their feelings are still real. If your actions

caused pain;even unintentionally;acknowledge that pain. It's not about proving intent. It's about valuing the heart of the one you love.

Forgiveness Must Be Final

When someone confesses a wrong - whether a small mistake or a deep betrayal - forgiveness must be genuine. That means it's not something we continue to bring up later in arguments. It's not something we remind them of to gain moral high ground.

I speak from experience. As I mentioned before, our marriage hit a crisis many years ago. We walked through a long, painful road of restoration. And by God's grace, we're still here. We're stronger. But I'll tell you;there were many moments when we wanted to throw that hurt back in each other's face, especially in future arguments. "Yes, I messed up dinner;but *you*..." That temptation is real.

But forgiveness, real forgiveness, requires that we don't keep weaponizing past hurts.

If Jesus stood before us daily and listed out every offense we'd committed;every moment of selfishness, cruelty, indifference;we wouldn't survive it. He said, "It is finished." He meant it. If we claim His grace, we must reflect it.

Especially in marriage.

Stop the Nagging; You're Not Parenting Each Other

Let's talk about nagging. We've heard from so many couples who say, "I feel like she talks to me like I'm one of the kids," or "He treats me like I don't know anything." That tone;condescending, sharp, or shaming;can slowly dismantle a relationship.

There's a big difference between saying, "Hey babe, I really need your help with the trash today. Do you have a minute to take care of that?" versus "I can't believe you didn't take out the trash again. You never help around here."

One is communication. The other is criticism.

Your spouse is not your child. Speak to them with respect. Even in frustration, choose words that build rather than break. That includes the way you approach daily differences.

Don't Blame. Don't Criticize. Encourage Instead.

It's easy to cast blame in the moment: "Where's my folder?" "I didn't move it." "You're the only one who touches it!"

We all do this in the small things. But here's the warning: if you don't learn how to hold space for grace in the little conflicts, you won't be prepared for the big ones.

What happens if tragedy strikes? What if a split-second mistake leads to real consequences;an accident, a lost job, a financial disaster? If your pattern is to blame in the small, you'll blame in the big;and it may destroy the bond that could have carried you through.

Use the small stuff as a training ground. Practice restoration. Build the habit of edifying your spouse, not tearing them down.

If You're Attacked - Don't Retaliate

Again - This does ***not*** apply to abuse. As I mentioned before, if you are in an emotionally, verbally, or physically abusive relationship, please talk to someone you trust. Abuse is never okay, and there are resources and people who can help.

But in the case of everyday marital conflict, when your spouse is upset and says something sharp or blaming, resist the urge to respond in kind. De-escalation is often the difference between a heated moment and a lasting wound. You don't always have to have the last word. Sometimes, humility is the most powerful answer.

Make Room for Differences

We all do life differently;and it shows up in the smallest ways.

For example, I can sleep in a bed that looks like it just came out of a toddler's pillow fight. Lights on, blankets askew - I'm out cold. Gregg, on the other hand, needs everything just right: lights off, even the tiniest LED covered, and sheets smoothed.

There were years when I would passive-aggressively grumble as he straightened the bed. We didn't *say* anything, but our body language screamed disapproval. Over time, I realized: does it really matter? Why not just make space for his preferences?

Gregg has shown the same grace. Like the lights I leave on in every single room of the house. It drives him nuts. But instead of snapping, he has adjusted to just getting up and turning them off himself. That's love in action.

The small things matter. If we allow space for differences with kindness, we avoid criticism, nagging, and conflict over things that;honestly, aren't eternal.

Be Concerned About Each Other's Interests

True communication starts long before the argument. I encourage you;take this list of principles and sit down together when things are *good*. Not during conflict. During peace. Go through each of the items. Ask yourselves:

- Which ones do I struggle with?
- Which ones do *you* notice I fall into?
- How can we plan ahead to do better next time?

We even had little signals for each other. Thinking back to the example I gave before about Gregg saying "but" after his apologies. We eventually sat down, and he said, "Ok, I don't even think I'm that aware that I'm doing it. So everytime I say "but" I want you to make a "T" with your hands to show me that I said it." So when Gregg used to say "but" in apologies, I'd make a "T" with my hands;timeout. That one gesture helped him become aware of something he was unaware of. But it was not me just pointing out his "mistake" - he had been the one to bring it up and had asked me to bring that awareness to him. And over time, with grace and repetition, that habit changed.

Awareness is half the battle. Practice makes progress.

The Art of Listening

Being a good communicator starts with being a great listener. Focus not just on *how* something is said, but *what* is being said. Don't get so caught up in your spouse's tone or expression that you miss their heart.

Sometimes the delivery is imperfect, but the message is honest.

Seek understanding. Extend grace. Choose humility.

In the end, our goal in marriage isn't to win the argument; it's to protect the relationship. Let me explain this a little better, using the analogy of a business. There are two business partners and the business entity itself. There might be times where the business partners get frustrated with each other, or don't see eye to eye on something - but at the end of the day they will work through the issue to choose what's best for the business and the mutually agreed upon definition of what that is. With marriage, if you think of it NOT just as the two of you, but as you, your spouse and the marriage covenant/entity itself - it helps to keep the focus on the commitment, and work through the short term frustration. Always keeping in mind the mutually agreed upon covenant you both made vs. winning the argument in front of you. Fighting for your marriage every day - more than you fight to be right - is worth everything.

Communication that Connects

Communication is the lifeblood of any relationship, especially marriage. It's how we share our hearts, solve problems, and stay connected. And yet, it's one of the areas that causes the most confusion, frustration, and pain, often not because we don't talk, but because we don't understand how we're communicating.

Let's begin with something as simple as a cookie.

The Cookie Test: What Defensiveness Reveals

Picture this: one of your kids walks into the kitchen, sees a batch of cookies, and grabs one. You come in and ask, "Did you take a cookie?" If they genuinely thought they were allowed to have one, they'll answer easily: "Yeah, I took one." No guilt, no anxiety. They're honest because they felt no need to hide.

But if you had previously said, "You may not have any of these cookies," and they still took one;and then you ask, "Did you take a cookie?"; you'll likely witness an entirely different response: "What? No. Why are you asking me that? I didn't take one. Maybe it was…" They might even point at crumbs and insist it wasn't them.

Defensiveness usually means there's something deeper going on. The same dynamic plays out in marriage. If your spouse says, "I can't believe you're talking to me like that," and your immediate response is, "I'm not talking to you like anything!" chances are… you probably are.

That moment of defensiveness? It's a gift. A mirror. A learning opportunity.

Instead of escalating, ask yourself: *Why am I getting defensive right now? What about this interaction is triggering me?* Often, it's not even about the current conversation. It might be an unresolved issue from the past, a sore spot in your story, or an insecurity that's been stirred up.

If you take the time to pause and explore the reason behind your defensiveness, you will learn something powerful about yourself. I've done this repeatedly, and it's still one of the most transformational habits I've built into my own life:

Ask, Don't Accuse

When conflict arises, focus on questions, not accusations. Seek understanding rather than rushing to judgment.

Let's illustrate this with a short, fun listening exercise.

The Bus Driver Test: Are You Really Listening?

Grab a pen. Take notes on what I say without turning the page. Ready?

You're driving a bus.

- At the first stop, six people get on.
- At the next stop, two more get on, and two get off.
- Then five get on, one gets off.
- Then two on, two off. This happens two more times.
- Finally, one person gets off at the last stop.

Here's the question: *How old is the bus driver?*

Got your answer?

Well, *you* are the bus driver. So how old are you?

If you missed it, you probably focused on counting passengers, not listening to the first sentence.

That's how it works in real life too. In conversations, especially emotional ones, we often miss the first thing someone says. We're already thinking about what we want to say next, or how to defend ourselves, or how to fix the problem. But communication starts with real, active listening.

Verbal and Non-Verbal Communication

Most of us think that communication is about the words we say. But, in reality, words are just a small part of it.

- **7%** of our communication is the actual words.
- **38%** is tone of voice.
- **55%** is body language.

Your facial expression, eye contact, tone, posture, and even your silence all send powerful messages. That's why two people can say "I'm fine" and mean completely opposite things.

And that's also why trying to have emotionally charged conversations over **text** or **email** is almost always a mistake.

You can't read tone through a screen. You don't see the eyes behind the words. You miss half the message, or worse, misinterpret it completely. We've worked with countless couples who've come to us hurt, not because of what was said, but because of how it was *misunderstood* over text.

If you're struggling to say something hard, and you don't feel brave enough to speak it aloud yet, consider writing a letter;but **read it in person**. Sit face-to-face. Let your body language, tone, and presence help convey what your heart wants to say.

And please – don't settle for sending a heavy text and calling it communication.

Practical Ground Rules for Tough Conversations

Here's a list of communication rules to consider adopting in your relationship. These aren't laws. They're tools to build safety, clarity, and intimacy:

1. **Do not raise voices.**
2. **Do not drag in past offenses.**
3. **Do not criticize.**
4. **Do not show contempt.**
5. **Do not become defensive.**
6. **Do not stonewall; practice reflective listening.**
7. **Stick to one issue at a time.**
8. **Focus on the problem, not the person.**
9. **Focus on the behavior, not the character.**
10. **Be specific, not general.**
11. **Express feelings instead of judging character.**

(Here's a piece of wisdom my mother gave me before I got married: She said, "No matter how hard things get, never attack your husband's core." You can say, *"I'm angry you lied about this,"* but don't say, *"You are a liar."*

That difference is everything. One addresses the action. The other cuts into a person's identity, creating deep wounds that are hard to heal. When someone attacks your core, it sticks. It lingers long after the argument is over. That one principle protected our foundation.)

12. **Observe facts; don't assume motives.**
13. **Seek mutual understanding, not victory.**
14. **Let go of the need for the last word.**
15. **Aim to grow closer, not just be right.**
16. **Seek forgiveness and move forward.**
17. **Don't solve problems that were never yours to solve.**

Let me explain that last one.

Sometimes, Just Listen

Not every problem needs a solution, at least not right away. Sometimes, your spouse just needs to vent. They need to feel heard, not fixed.

If you're not sure what they need, ask: "Do you want help, or do you just want me to listen?"

And if you're the one sharing, try saying: "I just need to vent right now. I don't need advice yet."

That small distinction can prevent a mountain of misunderstanding. It gives both of you permission to show up without pressure and to support one another in the way that's actually helpful.

I remember distinctly when our kids were young and Gregg worked from home. Some days were just long with 3 young children so I would go into his office and start complaining about something. Immediately he would "suggest" a better way to do what I had been doing or how to handle the kids better. I would feel so furious and unsupported - and would feel like he questioned my ability to be a good mother. Once we specified that I would start the conversation with "I'm here to vent" or "I'm here for some advice" - it changed everything. We even defined what would be helpful for me to hear if I'm simply venting. So then, when I would vent, he would simply stand up - give me a long hug and say, "You are a great mom - I'm sorry it's been frustrating, but you've got this". That simple action left me feeling supported and seen.

Healthy communication can be so much easier if we take the time to DEFINE our needs to our spouse and then actually put those into practice!

The Nail in the Head

You may have seen the viral video called *"It's Not About the Nail."* In it, a woman, with a nail sticking out of her head is describing how overwhelmed she feels with a pressure in her head. The man, seeing an obvious nail stuck in her forehead, keeps suggesting she remove it. But she insists: "It's not about the nail. I just need you to listen."

It's exaggerated;but only slightly.

So many conversations in marriage go sideways because one person just wants empathy, while the other jumps into problem-solving mode. Don't be the fixer when your spouse just needs a friend.

The Choice is Yours

Communication is a skill, not a personality trait. It's something you can practice, grow in, and refine over time. But the real secret?

It's a choice.

A choice to slow down. A choice to listen. A choice to be kind, even when you're frustrated. A choice to use words that build up instead of tear down.

You're reading this chapter because something inside you wants to make marriage better. You want a connection. You want healing. You want more.

And it starts here – with the way you speak, the way you listen, and the way you choose to love even when the conversation is hard.

Don't let this chapter collect dust.

Let it change the way you talk to the person you love.

1. How do you typically respond to conflict in your marriage, and how might your habits impact your spouse and family?
2. Are there areas where you struggle to admit when you are wrong, and how could practicing genuine apologies transform your relationship?
3. How do you currently handle past offenses: do you bring them up repeatedly, or are you able to forgive and move forward fully?
4. In what ways do you listen to your spouse: do you listen to understand, or do you often respond defensively or try to fix things immediately?
5. How can you create intentional communication practices that honor differences, avoid blame or criticism, and foster connection even during disagreements?

CHAPTER 11

Reclaiming Intimacy:

Communication, Vulnerability, and God's Design of Sex

There's Always Room for Growth

Marriage is not a destination. It's a journey of continual growth. Just when you think you've mastered one area, a new challenge arises. Maybe you've gotten better at managing conflict, but now you find it hard to express affection. That's okay. Because at the core of every lasting marriage is the power of choice. We get to choose growth. We get to choose connection. And each morning, you can wake up and say, "I want my marriage to be great." Because it can be.

A thriving marriage doesn't require perfection. Iit requires practice. Practice, practice, practice. Communication, conflict resolution, understanding. None of these are one-time achievements. They are lifelong disciplines. And when we are intentional, when we make the choice daily to pursue one another, everything begins to change.

The Power of Observation

To drive this point home, we have led couples through a simple but eye-opening exercise: Partners stood facing each other, just a few feet apart, and observed one another from head to toe. Then, backs were turned, and each person made three subtle or obvious changes to their appearance. When they turned back around, their partner had to guess what had changed.

It sounds simple, even silly, but the lesson can be profound. How well do we really know the details of our spouse? Do we take the time to notice small changes, small needs, small signals? So often, we get swept into the busyness of life and miss the beautiful, subtle shifts in the person we love most.

Take note. Look up. Notice. Whether it's a new shirt or a subtle change in mood, when we pay attention to the small things, we build intimacy in ways that words alone never could.

Understanding True Intimacy

When most people hear the word "intimacy," their minds jump straight to sex. And yes, sexual intimacy is part of a healthy marriage. But, it's only one part. True intimacy in marriage involves four vital dimensions:

1. **Communication** – Honest conversations, active listening, and managing disagreements. All of these create space for deeper connection. Even conflict, when navigated well, can be a catalyst for closeness.
2. **Friendship** – Shared memories, laughter, adventure, and mutual support form the backbone of a thriving marriage. Friendship

invites joy and reminds us that love can be fun.

3. **Spirituality** – Praying together, reading scripture, worshiping, and serving side by side unite couples in purpose and in faith. This form of intimacy may feel awkward at first, especially for those with different backgrounds, but it can become one of the strongest bonds in a marriage.

4. **Sexuality** – Flirting, touch, and sexual connection all build a level of trust and pleasure that deepens emotional and physical connection. But sexual intimacy thrives best when the other forms of intimacy are nurtured.

What binds all four dimensions together? **Vulnerability.**

Without vulnerability, we hit a wall. We can't truly be seen or known. Vulnerability in communication, friendship, spirituality, and sexuality opens the doors to deep, soul-level connection.

Top 10 Intimacy Needs

To help couples evaluate where they stand in these areas, here are ten core intimacy needs. Reflect on these together:

- **Acceptance** – Am I loved as I am?
- **Affection** – Is love expressed through touch and presence?

- **Appreciation** – Are my efforts noticed and valued?
- **Approval** – Do I feel affirmed and supported?
- **Attention** – Do we pay attention to each other's needs?
- **Comfort and Empathy** – Do we offer safe space for pain?
- **Encouragement** – Do we inspire each other toward growth?
- **Respect** – Do we honor each other's perspectives and boundaries?
- **Security** – Is this relationship a refuge?
- **Support** – Are we a team through the highs and lows?

Without these foundational needs being met, intimacy becomes difficult. But with intentional effort, couples can meet each other's needs and foster a deep, abiding connection.

Sex Is a Gift; Not a Taboo

Let's reclaim what God designed. Sex is not a dirty word. It's not a secret shame. It is a beautiful, God-ordained part of marriage meant for joy, unity, and even health.

Consider these ten health benefits of sex:

1. **Improves the immune system**
2. **Boosts libido**
3. **Strengthens bladder control in women**

4. **Lowers blood pressure**
5. **Increases energy**
6. **Boosts self-esteem**
7. **Burns calories (about 4 per minute!)**
8. **Lowers the risk of heart disease**
9. **Provides pain relief**
10. **Reduces the risk of prostate cancer**

Sex is also God's gift for connection:

- **Procreation** – "Be fruitful and multiply" (Genesis 1:28).
- **Unity** – "The two shall become one flesh" (Mark 10:6-9).
- **Pleasure** – An entire book of the Bible (Song of Songs) celebrates it!

God's design for sex involves physical pleasure, emotional bonding, spiritual unity, and mutual giving. When done God's way, in a covenant of love and trust, it brings joy, not shame.

Naked and Unashamed

Genesis 2:25 says, "Adam and his wife were both naked, and they felt no shame." That verse captures the heart of God's intent for marital intimacy. Not just physical nakedness but emotional transparency. The ability to be completely open, completely known, and still completely loved.

This kind of intimacy requires more than attraction. It requires trust, humility, patience, and effort. It's a lifelong journey of getting to know and love your spouse more deeply each day.

One Flesh, One Spirit, One Purpose

God's vision for marriage is not just survival, it's oneness. One flesh. One spirit. One purpose. Through open communication, playful friendship, shared faith, and joyful sex, a couple becomes more than two people living side by side; they become a united team, deeply bonded in heart and soul.

So start small. Pay attention. Be honest. Be vulnerable. Practice every day. And trust that with God's help, your marriage can grow into something beautiful, whole, and deeply intimate.

Intimacy Without Shame ; Reclaiming God's Design for Sex in Marriage

"And the man and his wife were both naked and were not ashamed." - Genesis 2:25

Something deeply spiritual and sacred happens when a husband and wife come together in sexual intimacy. God designed sex not just for reproduction, but for pleasure, connection, oneness, and renewal in the covenant of marriage. Yet, so many Christian couples struggle in this area; not for lack of desire, but because of fear, shame, disappointment, or silence.

I want to have this conversation not to provoke discomfort, but to invite freedom. God is not embarrassed by sex. He created it. The enemy, however, has worked overtime to distort it, shame it, and confuse it. My goal in this chapter is to reclaim God's vision for intimacy by offering grace-filled clarity and practical tools for building a safe, joyful, and holy sex life in your marriage.

1. Sex Isn't Everything, But It Is Significant

Let's start here: sex isn't the foundation of your marriage, but it is a significant part of it. It's a form of communication, a language that speaks affection, trust, vulnerability, and joy.

If this area is completely dead or avoided, something else in the marriage is likely suffering. Often, lack of sexual intimacy isn't the root issue but a symptom of emotional distance, exhaustion, insecurity, conflict, or unmet needs. Just like an engine light, a dwindling sex life is a signal - it tells you to pay attention and care for each other more deeply.

2. Healthy Communication Unlocks Intimacy

We've sat with so many couples who are stuck simply because they haven't talked honestly about their sexual relationship. Maybe they assumed they were "on the same page." Or maybe one partner carries a sense of inadequacy, and the other feels unwanted. Or maybe, like many, they just don't have a vocabulary for this kind of conversation.

Start here: Can we talk about our sex life without embarrassment or fear?

Ask each other:

- What makes you feel most emotionally connected to me?
- What does a fulfilling sex life look like to you?
- Is there anything I do that makes you feel pursued or rejected?
- Is there any shame or past pain that's still affecting how we approach sex?

Give each other space to share and listen without defensiveness. Approach each other with the humility of learners and the commitment of lovers.

3. Drop the Baggage, Pick Up Grace

Too many believers drag shame into the bedroom. Some carry trauma, others carry church-based guilt. Some men grew up with porn and now struggle with unrealistic expectations. Some women were taught that sex is "just for him" and feel used or unseen. Others were sexually active before marriage and now feel disqualified from experiencing God's blessing.

Let me say it clearly: if you are in Christ, your past is forgiven. There is no condemnation. Your marriage bed can be a place of restoration - not punishment.

Hebrews 13:4 says, "Let marriage be held in honor among all, and let the marriage bed be undefiled." That word *undefiled* means not stained or polluted. It doesn't mean perfect. It means whole, clean, and sacred. If something is defiling your intimacy, whether it's pornography, bitterness, fear, or unresolved pain, it's time to invite the Lord into that space and begin healing.

4. Give Each Other the Gift of Safety

Great sex doesn't begin in the bedroom - it begins with emotional safety. When a spouse feels judged, ignored, or pressured, their heart shuts down. When a spouse feels cherished, known, and free to say no or yes without guilt, they can relax and engage.

Here's a good rule: never use sex as a reward or punishment.

This is not about manipulation or obligation, it's about mutual generosity. The Bible says in 1 Corinthians 7 that each spouse has authority over the other's body, not as a weapon, but as a sign of belonging. We are meant to give, not take; to bless, not pressure.

Pray together. Check in regularly. Stay connected emotionally, spiritually, and physically. The more trust you build outside the bedroom, the more joy you'll find inside it.

5. Attraction Is More Than Skin Deep

We live in a culture obsessed with appearance. But real sexual attraction in marriage grows deeper than physical form. It's rooted in attentiveness, kindness, energy, and pursuit.

Husbands, your wife needs to feel seen, heard, and safe in order to feel sexual desire. If she's exhausted, emotionally depleted, or feeling dismissed, it's likely that her body will shut down too.

Wives, your husband needs to feel respected, affirmed, and desired, not just needed. If he senses rejection or coldness, he may internalize it as failure or disconnection.

Attraction is cultivated. That means choosing to notice one another, to flirt again, to give attention to the little things: eye contact, a playful touch, an affectionate compliment, a kind tone. And yes, physical self-care matters too - not out of pressure, but because loving and caring for your body is one way of honoring your spouse.

6. Deal With the Distractions

Life is full of things that crowd out intimacy: kids, work, screens, stress, fatigue. If you're waiting for a moment where both of you feel rested, excited, and unbothered... you might be waiting a while.

Make room for intimacy. Prioritize it. It doesn't have to be a grand production; sometimes it's just carving out twenty minutes for connection, slowing down enough to look each other in the eye, or scheduling a night where you leave your phones outside the room.

Sex is not just spontaneous. It can be sacred and scheduled too. Be intentional.

7. Let God In

For many couples, sex is the only area they haven't prayed about. They pray about finances, parenting, health... but never think to invite the Holy Spirit into their bedroom. But, He's not embarrassed or absent. He's invested in every part of your marriage.

Invite Him to teach you how to love one another better. Ask for healing where there's pain. Ask for freedom where there's shame. Ask for creativity, joy, and laughter where there's been stress.

Sex is not dirty. It's holy. And when it's cherished in covenant, it becomes a place of worship.

8. Keep Pursuing, Keep Growing

No marriage has "arrived" in the area of intimacy. You don't have to be perfect. You just have to be willing. Talk about it. Laugh about it. Learn together. Give each other grace.

And most of all, remember that sex is not just about the act. It's about the *union*. It's about making space for each other again and again. It's about rediscovering what makes your love unique and sacred.

Let your marriage bed be a place of truth, tenderness, and trust. Not just for tonight, but for a lifetime.

The master bedroom is more than just a physical space. In marriage, it symbolizes the heart of vulnerability, trust, and connection. It's the place where deep intimacy – emotional, physical, and spiritual – can flourish. But it's also the place where fears, awkwardness, and insecurity can creep in. That's why it's essential to cultivate safety, grace, and open communication in this sacred part of your relationship.

So - remember ....

1. Give Yourself Permission to Make Mistakes

Trying something new in marriage, especially when it involves intimacy or communication, can feel clumsy at first. Maybe you've had awkward conversations, or tried to express a need or desire, and it didn't land well. That's okay.

Allow space for mistakes. Growth in marriage doesn't require perfection. It requires persistence. When you try new ways of connecting – emotionally or physically – it may feel unnatural at first. That doesn't mean it's wrong or broken. It means you're learning together.

Just like any new skill, meaningful connection takes practice. And practice involves missteps. Give one another grace as you explore new ways of talking, loving, and engaging. Laugh together when it's awkward. Reassure each other when it's messy. Keep trying.

"Love bears all things, believes all things, hopes all things, endures all things." – *1 Corinthians 13:7*

2. Talk About the Hard Things In Person

When it comes to emotionally loaded topics, especially related to intimacy, it's tempting to avoid direct conversations. But as stated earlier, texts and emails can only go so far. Tone gets lost. Nuance disappears. And misunderstandings multiply.

Hard conversations deserve face-to-face moments. Body language, eye contact, tone of voice...these matter deeply when you're navigating vulnerability. Even if it's uncomfortable, make space to sit together and talk. Be honest. Be present. And be willing to hear one another without defensiveness.

But here's the flip side...

3. Sometimes a Text Can Help Start the Conversation

Not all communication has to be heavy or serious. In fact, when things feel awkward or unfamiliar, sometimes a lighthearted message can break the ice. A flirty text, a thoughtful email, or even a handwritten love note can go a long way toward creating connection.

Written words can help you say the things that feel too hard to say out loud. Especially when it's about something positive, something you want to try, share, or express affection about. Writing it down can remove the pressure and invite playfulness.

So go ahead and send that silly text. Leave a love note on the bathroom mirror. Email a letter that shares your heart. These small gestures can soften walls and build bridges.

4. Make It Fun - Because God Designed Intimacy to Be Good

Let's not forget: this is supposed to be fun.

God didn't create intimacy as a duty or burden. It was His *good* idea from the beginning. Something to be enjoyed. Something to bond you. Something sacred and beautiful.

So go out and explore it - together. Laugh. Play. Try new things. Build emotional safety so that you can truly enjoy what God has given you as husband and wife. Don't let shame or past baggage steal the joy God intended.

"Every good and perfect gift is from above..." – *James 1:17*

5. Build a Safe Space for True Vulnerability

At the heart of it all, the greatest gift you can offer your spouse, especially in the "master bedroom" spaces of your relationship, is safety.

Always make one another feel safe, protected, loved, and understood. When these are in place, walls come down. Trust deepens. Vulnerability becomes possible. And with vulnerability comes true intimacy...not just physical, but emotional and spiritual as well.

Marriage isn't a sprint, it's a marathon. You won't always get it right, and neither will your spouse. But when you both keep practicing – coming back to the core tools of safety, grace, and open communication – you'll see powerful transformation over time.

We don't have perfect communication. We mess this up - often. But we keep coming back, keep trying again, keep laughing and learning together. That's what makes it beautiful.

And honestly? When couples start to apply this, not just talk about it, but actually *do* it, it's amazing what can happen. Walls come down. Conversations open up. Intimacy grows. Burdens are shared.

So talk about it. Especially the hard things. Especially the fun things. Build each other up. Be brave and tender and playful. And remember: this is a gift from God, one meant to be enjoyed, celebrated, and cherished.

Let the master bedroom be the place where safety thrives, vulnerability is welcomed, and love grows deeper every day.

Chapter 11 *Reflection Questions:*

1. How intentional am I in noticing the small changes, needs, or signals in my spouse, and how could increasing my attentiveness strengthen our intimacy?
2. Which of the four dimensions of intimacy – communication, friendship, spirituality, or sexuality – needs the most attention in my marriage right now, and what practical steps can I take to nurture it?
3. Are there past experiences, shame, or fear that are affecting how I approach sexual intimacy, and how can I invite God's grace to bring healing and freedom in this area?
4. How can I create a safe and playful space for vulnerability in my marriage, where both my spouse and I feel loved, understood, and free to express our desires and emotions?
5. In what ways can I practice daily choices, like listening, affirming, and showing affection, that build trust, emotional safety, and deeper connection with my spouse?

Part 4

KITCHEN

CHAPTER 12

Plan or Panic

The Kitchen – More Than Just Meals

Life often revolves around the kitchen. It's where we refuel, reconnect, and - sometimes - have our most ridiculous arguments. In our house, the kitchen is Gregg's favorite room, mostly because he loves food. But for many of us, it's also the hub of planning and preparing, not just meals, but the rhythm of family life. And if we're honest, sometimes that rhythm is more like a jazz solo: spontaneous, emotional, and prone to the occasional offbeat.

Planning or Panicking?

Every day, two things happen in the kitchen: we plan meals, and we prepare them. That sounds simple enough, but let's be real, I am not a natural meal planner. I'm more of a five-o'clock "Do we have eggs and toast?" kind of mom. I try. I do. But more often than not, I find myself scrambling, literally and figuratively.

And it's not just about the food. It's about life. Planning meals is often code for: how are we managing our time, our money, our expectations, our stress? How are we feeding ourselves and each other, not just nutritionally, but emotionally?

There is a great video that I have dubbed "The Chicken Wing Conflict" that many couples could relate to. In it, a husband and wife, full of humor and honesty, reenact a marital spat that started with something simple – dinner.

It begins with the husband calling his wife and suggesting they ditch the home cooked meal she had already planned and go out for chicken wings instead. His tone was casual, even playful. Her response? Less so.

"I've already taken my bra off," she replied.

And if you're laughing right now, you're probably married.

What followed was a surprisingly profound (and hilarious) unraveling of a very real and very relatable argument. What started as a debate about dinner quickly spiraled into a deeper tension around spontaneity, finances, and planning;something most couples know all too well.

The husband wanted to be spontaneous. The wife wanted structure. He imagined picking up wings and beers. She had already defrosted chicken and mentally checked out for the evening. From there, they escalated: Why don't we ever do fun things anymore? Why do you always over-plan? Why don't you care about our budget?

And suddenly, the fight was no longer about dinner – it was about everything.

Their pastor (also their marriage counselor) gave them the best advice: "Stay in Cleveland."

That phrase has stuck with me. Cleveland, in this analogy, is the original argument – the dinner, the chicken, the bra. The uncomfortable, annoying, seemingly trivial moment. But instead of staying there, we tend to board a metaphorical plane and fly to Chicago (Why don't you ever plan?) or L.A. (We have financial issues!) or New York (You never listen to me!).

His point was simple, but brilliant: If the argument starts in Cleveland, stay in Cleveland. Don't bring in every other unresolved issue. Handle the moment. Be present with what it really is. Because when we start adding in every city on the map, no argument gets resolved. We just end up emotionally jet-lagged.

Planning in Real Life

The truth is, planning is essential. Outside of marriage, we plan almost everything. Buying a house. Buying a car. Retirement. Schooling. Sports. Girls' night out. We don't just drive around hoping our friends show up at the same place. We plan, we coordinate, we commit.

So why is it that we often resist planning within our marriages? Why do we assume date nights, mealtimes, communication, and intimacy should just "happen"?

They don't. At least not consistently or healthily.

Even vacations, which are supposed to be relaxing, require planning. Not just where you're going, but what you want to do, what your expectations are, and how to handle potential stress. Otherwise, you end up frustrated in paradise.

The Deeper Message

The kitchen is a symbol. It represents how we nourish one another – physically, emotionally, and relationally. The mess, the prep, the dishes, the smells, the teamwork, the tension, the laughter, the "I've already taken my bra off" moments; all of it is real life.

We don't need perfection. We just need intention.

So, whether you're the spreadsheet scheduler or the "let's wing it" wanderer in your relationship, remember this: a little planning can go a long way, especially when paired with humor, grace, and maybe, occasionally, a plate of wings.

Well, God calls us to plan our lives. He gives us specific instructions in Scripture - how to act, how to speak, how to behave, how to plan. He shows us what kind of goals we should have, what our priorities should be, and what things are *not* priorities. He calls us to participate actively, not to sit on the sidelines. We're meant to step into the story. That requires a plan.

Scripture is full of stories about the importance of planning;and the consequences of failing to do so. Those who neglect planning are often described as foolish. Scripture talks about the wise and foolish builders in Matthew, the builder who counted the cost in Luke, the king who prepared for battle in Luke, and the unjust steward, also in Luke. Each of these stories highlights people who were given a task;but didn't prepare or plan, and it didn't go well for them.

So, how do we know if it's a *good* plan?

One helpful tool is the SMART acronym. SMART stands for:

- **Specific**
- **Measurable**
- **Attainable**
- **Relevant**
- **Time-bound**

Let's break that down.

Specific: Ask questions until there are no more questions to ask. For example, let's say someone tells you, "I like it when you give me hugs." That's a nice start, but it's not specific. So you ask, "How often? Once a day?" And they say, "Actually, I'd love one in the morning and one in the evening." Great, now we know it's two hugs a day. Then you ask, "How long should the hug be? Is it a quick pat or something more intentional?" And they say, "No, I want you to stop what you're doing, put your phone down, and hug me for a full 15 seconds." Now you're clear. That's a specific plan.

Same with things like "I'm working late tonight." Okay, but what does that mean? Do I keep dinner warm? Are you eating at the office? Should I wait up? There are so many questions that can be asked when something is left vague. Don't assume, ask. Be specific.

Measurable: There should be a clear outcome. What are we aiming for? What does "done" look like? If your plan doesn't have an obvious way to measure success, then how will you know you've achieved it?

Attainable: Be realistic. Sure, we'd all love to have $10 million, but is that attainable? Not likely, at least not overnight. Similarly, be mindful of emotional and time-related limitations. If it's a crazy week and you're both stretched thin, maybe aiming for two date nights isn't realistic.

Now, I do believe in setting high goals. Don't aim low! But make sure your goal is *attainable*, even if it takes five years. If it's too much for right now, that's okay. Adjust the time frame. But don't set yourselves up for failure.

Relevant: We'll talk more in other chapters about family mission statements and personal values. When you're setting goals, ask yourself: *Is this in line with our purpose? Does it reflect who we are, who we want to become, and what matters most to us as a family?*

Don't chase goals that have nothing to do with your real life. That said, if it's about friendships, for example, that *is* relevant, because friends are part of your life. Just make sure your goals connect with your values.

Time-bound: Your goals need a timeline. You should be able to look back in six months or a year and ask: *Did we do it?* If not, why not? Did the goal change? Was it no longer a priority? That's fine. But maybe the issue was that you didn't plan well or didn't follow through. Timelines help you track, adjust, and plan next steps.

Now, you might be thinking: "Okay, but how are we supposed to do all this? We're so busy! The kids, work, the travel schedule... when are we supposed to plan?" I get it. Our life is crazy, too. But this doesn't have to be overwhelming. It doesn't have to happen every day, or even every week for certain goals; but you *can* set yourself up for success.

Start by scheduling the time.

And a tip: *don't* try to plan at night. I don't know about you, but by the time our kids are in bed, we are exhausted. That is *not* a good time to sit down and plan. I might be there physically, but mentally? I'm toast. That's my time to watch something silly or wind down, not to engage in serious conversations.

So don't try to cram goal setting into the end of a long day. If your living room is your chill zone, and you don't want to turn it into a boardroom, then choose another space, like the kitchen table. And schedule it: "Hey, on Wednesday at 7:30 p.m., let's sit down for 20 minutes and talk about this." Put it in the calendar and treat it like a real meeting.

Make it a priority.
This won't happen by accident. You have to choose to make it a priority. Think about work – you wouldn't just skip meetings with your boss or forget to plan your projects. You'd lose your job. Yet in marriage, we sometimes think, "It's fine, it's just my spouse." But long-term, that thinking chips away at respect and connection.

Remove distractions.
And I don't just mean your kids. You can plan while they're asleep. I mean phones, background TV, music, even things like the washing machine buzzer. If you know something's going to pull your focus, take care of it beforehand. Turn off your phone. It's okay. No one will die if it's off for 30 minutes. I know the temptation. I once almost drove home from the store just to get my phone before buying one item. But we have to break that attachment in these moments. Be present.

Now, let's talk about two types of planning: long-term and short-term.

Long-Term Plans

These are things you might talk about once or twice a year. We'll carve out a few days and say, "Okay, this week, we're doing our planning." Then we'll assign certain topics to specific days: Monday we talk about one area, Tuesday another, and so on.

We'll schedule out and talk about different topics on different days, and not at home. Why? Because it's easy to get overwhelmed and distracted. We make it intentional by setting a specific time and place, usually outside the home, so it feels more like a business meeting. It has a sense of focus and importance. For us, summertime is ideal. It lines up with our wedding anniversary, so it feels like a natural "new year" to reflect and reset.

Here are the key areas we review together at least once a year. I encourage you to consider them as conversation starters for your own planning time:

1. Spiritual

We ask each other honestly: *How are you doing spiritually?* Are we giving each other space to grow? Sometimes we'll use a scale of 1 to 10 just to give a sense of where we are. You can talk about it openly or use some kind of metric. It's really about creating a shared awareness.

2. Marriage

This deserves its own category and usually its own planning session. We break it down into areas like:

- **Intimacy**
- **Communication**
- **Conflict resolution**
- **Shared time**

Are we connecting? Are we thriving or just coasting? The key is openness without judgment.

3. Parenting

This changes fast as the kids grow. Seasons of life bring new dynamics: elementary school vs. middle school vs. high school vs. college, sports seasons, social changes, preparing for college. We take time to ask:

- Are we on the same page?
- Do we need to adjust our approach?
- What are the current struggles or successes?

4. Work & Career

Even if you've been in the same job for decades, this question matters:

- Do you still enjoy your work?
- What's changing?
- Are there areas of burnout or boredom?
- Do we need to adjust travel, workload, or time off?

5. Finances

This is an incredibly important topic and needs to be addressed. Talk about:

- Budgeting
- Saving
- Debt
- Retirement
- College planning
- Big upcoming expenses

You may feel "set" financially, but if you haven't talked about it together, you're probably not as aligned as you think.

6. Health

Check in on physical wellness, not just illness.

- Are we eating well?
- Are we exercising?
- Are we modeling healthy habits for our kids?

It doesn't have to be about gym memberships. It could be just committing to nightly walks together.

7. Ministry & Service

Serving others is vital, but overcommitting can cause stress and take away from family. So we ask:

- Are we doing too much?
- Are we doing too little?
- What needs to shift?

Ministry should never replace the mission of family. It should enhance it.

8. Travel

My family loves to travel, and we've realized we need to plan for it. Our kids are getting older, and we want to make memories before they leave the house. Even if it's a trip a few years out, we need to start planning now.

9. Fun

Fun doesn't just happen. It has to be planned, or it gets squeezed out. So we ask:

- What's something fun we want to do this year?
- What are *attainable* things that would bring joy?

Even something small like "go on a bike ride together" can be missed if it never gets named.

All of these topics can feel like a lot. So, if this seems overwhelming, here's the encouragement: **Just start somewhere.** You don't have to tackle everything all at once. Choose one area, one topic, one goal. Think of it like learning a new skill: riding a bike, cooking, swimming. You can't do it all in one week, but over time it becomes natural.

Some of you may be planners by nature. This structure might feel exciting. Others may never have had a goal-setting conversation in your marriage or even in your life. That's okay. Just start with one intentional conversation.

*** Also, remember that if you feel stuck in any one of these areas specifically - maybe you are in a bad place financially and you don't know how to fix it, or you feel like parenting is not going well and your kids are out of control ... GET HELP. Sometimes these "planning sessions" bring to light areas that really need renovation and where outside help is crucial. Reach out. Get experts* *involved. Each of these areas needs to be functioning effectively for your home to feel safe and secure. ***

And to help with that, we've included a **Strategic Planning Cycle**. This is something I pulled from my business background, and I think it fits beautifully in the home context.

The Strategic Planning Cycle

In the center of the model is your **mission**. We'll talk about creating that mission statement later. Everything else flows from that.

1. **Set Goals**
   Where do we want to go from here?
2. **Strategize**
   What are the paths we could take? What's realistic?
3. **Identify Targets**
   What are the measurable outcomes?
4. **Review Progress**
   Six months or a year from now - how did we do?
5. **Evaluate & Adjust**
   What do we change? What worked well?

This model works not just for business, but for marriage, family, and life. It keeps your conversations from being just emotional or reactive. It helps you track real progress.

So, my challenge for you today: **Put a date on the calendar.** Even if it's three or six months from now, set a day for this conversation. That's the first act of leadership – protecting space for what matters.

Next, we'll talk about short-term or weekly planning. I know, it might sound like a lot. You may be thinking, "We don't even have time to eat dinner together, how are we going to plan each week? That's fair. But let me encourage you that this isn't about perfection. It's about building a habit. Think of this section as "training wheels." We'll walk through the three categories of weekly planning next. Now, you might be somebody who, if this is something new to you, needs to *choose a time* for this. When we started doing it, we chose Sunday nights. After the kids were in bed, we said, "Okay, we're going to sit down for half an hour or an hour," and we'd go through these areas each week.

Now, for us, we don't just do Sunday nights anymore. It's like bike riding. It's just become something that's easier, more natural. We now do this kind of on a daily basis. We'll ask each other some of these questions casually. It doesn't feel so forced, like it did at the very beginning.

So, if it feels forced when you first start, that's *completely okay*. Still sit down, pick a time, and have a meeting.

1. How does your approach to planning (or lack of it) affect the rhythm and emotional climate of your home and marriage?
2. Think of a recent disagreement in your household: did you "stay in Cleveland" or did the argument escalate to other issues? How could staying present have changed the outcome?
3. Which areas of your life (spiritual, marriage, parenting, finances, health, fun, etc.) would benefit most from intentional long-term planning?
4. How do distractions or fatigue impact your ability to plan effectively, and what practical steps could you take to create focused, intentional planning time?
5. How can you apply the SMART goals framework to set realistic, meaningful plans for your family or marriage, and what would be a first step toward implementing it?

CHAPTER 13

Logistical, Emotional and Practical Planning

Three categories are covered on a regular basis: logistical, emotional, and practical.

Let's start with **logistical planning**. This is the typical "get-through-the-week" kind of planning most of us already do. It's the calendar check-in: "What's happening this week? Where do I need to be? What's out of the ordinary? Who's driving the kids to practice? Are you out of town? When are you leaving? Do I need to drop you at the airport?"

It's that kind of stuff.

And a lot of us already do it – kind of. But some of us don't look ahead. So we get to Wednesday afternoon and suddenly your husband's working late, and you're like, "Wait, what? I made dinner. I invited friends over. You're not coming?"

He says, "Oh, sorry. I forgot to tell you."

And you're upset. Totally understandable. That kind of thing happens *all the time.*

But if you had sat down on Sunday and said, "Hey, by the way, I was thinking of inviting friends over on Wednesday to have dinner with us," he could've said, "Oh, actually, I'll be working late," and you could have saved the argument and the disappointment.

It's not the *big things* that derail us. It's often the small logistical stuff that builds up. If you don't talk about it ahead of time, it can cause arguments, tension, and resentment.

Once you've done logistical planning, then you move into what I call **Emotional Strategic Planning**, which is *so important* in marriage.

Now I know, as soon as I say "emotional planning," I lose some of you. You're thinking, "Nope, not for me." And that's okay. But hear me out - this doesn't mean you have to sit around crying and talking about your childhood. This is still a *planning* session.

What I mean by the emotional side is: *What might affect us emotionally this week?*

Maybe someone's traveling. Maybe there's a big business proposal due. Maybe, for a stay-at-home mom, it's tech week for the school play and the schedule is insane. Maybe your kid is graduating. That kind of stuff affects us emotionally, whether we talk about it or not.

So, if someone says, "Hey, I've got a huge presentation Thursday. I'm stressed," that's helpful. The other person can now say, "Okay, how can I support you? What would help make that easier?" Maybe your spouse is working late. Instead of being annoyed, you say, "You know what? I'll bring you dinner to the office so you don't have to leave."

That's a completely different outcome than, "You're what? You're working late? I made dinner!"

It changes *everything*. One scenario causes tension. The other shows love and support.

So, yes - emotional planning matters. A few questions you can ask each other:

- What can I do to make you feel loved this week?
- How can I encourage you?
- What are you worried about this week?
- What are you excited about?
- What can I do to make you feel proud or supported?
- How can I make your week easier?

Now listen - some of your husbands don't love the emotional questions. I get it. Mine doesn't either. But if I ask, "What can I do to make your week easier?" - he *will* give me something. That's a great entry point to emotional support, especially for people who don't naturally lean into emotion.

This also applies to *out-of-the-ordinary* things.

Let me give you an example. Gregg's family lives in Pennsylvania. We used to live in Virginia, then spent a year in PA near his family. Gregg has *30 cousins*, on one side. So, it's a big family. And they do reunions.

I don't love reunions. I don't know most of the extended family, and some of them ask me

questions like, "Did you ride elephants in Africa?"
(Yes, that's a real example.)

So every year, we'd go. I'd feel overwhelmed, uncomfortable, left with random relatives while Gregg caught up with cousins. And every year, we'd fight on the way home. I felt unseen and unsupported. He felt like I wasn't enjoying his family. It was so unnecessary.

Until we started planning for it.

One year, we sat down and said, "What are we trying to *get* out of this day?" He said, "I want to connect with these three cousins, be there for lunch, and stay until 3:30 or 4pm."

I said, "Okay. But I need you to be aware of me. If you see me stuck in a long convo with a random aunt, help me out. Come join or rescue me."

And also, I told him, "*You* need to be the one to say it's time to leave, not me. Otherwise, I look like the in-law who's dragging us away."

So he did. We had a great time. We high-fived in the car afterward because for the first time in years, we *didn't have an argument* after a reunion.

That's the power of emotional planning. You look at upcoming events - especially the out-of-the-ordinary ones - and you ask:

What are your expectations?

What are my triggers?

What can we agree on ahead of time so we *both* feel supported?

When summer comes, that means camps, trips, schedule changes. Start talking about:

- What camps are we doing?
- Are the kids doing sports?
- When are we traveling?
- How long are we staying?
- Who are we visiting?
- What are our expectations for those visits?

Don't just assume you're on the same page. Talk it out.

These conversations aren't just practical, they're powerful. They build trust, reduce conflict, and set you up to thrive instead of just surviving.

Planning for Peace - Aligning Expectations in the Everyday

Have you ever planned an entire summer in your mind without ever voicing it? Maybe you envisioned your kids in Vacation Bible School and just one or two camps, hoping to preserve free time. Meanwhile, your partner was banking on a full schedule of sports camps to get a jump on next season. If you've experienced a moment like this, you're not alone.

Many couples assume their plans are understood. Or worse, identical. But silent expectations often collide loudly. We enter seasons like summer or holidays with completely different priorities and ideas about where we'll go, who we'll see, and how we'll spend our time. The result? Misunderstandings, tension, and disappointment.

To avoid this, we need to plan proactively and communicate intentionally.

Protecting Time, Protecting Peace

In our home, summer can quickly fill up with visits from friends and family. I tend to be the "we-have-an-open-room-so-why-not?" type. But my husband? He needs downtime and space to decompress. If we don't talk in advance about who's coming and when, we run the risk of overscheduling and burning out.

So we started blocking weeks on our calendar: visitor weeks and "protected" weeks. This simple act of planning transformed our summer rhythm and helped us respect one another's limits. So, create protected time on your calendar where no guests, activities, or big obligations are allowed. Use this time for rest and reconnection.

The Power of the 3x5 Note Card

Yes, it might feel forced. But new habits often do. Like riding a bike or learning to swim, building rhythms of connection takes some intentional awkwardness at first.

That's why I suggest a 3x5 note card for planning!
On one side, we focus on logistics. On the other,
emotional needs.

Side One: Logistical Expectations

These are the nuts and bolts of your upcoming
week:

- Who's picking up the kids?
- What appointments are scheduled?
- Is anyone traveling?
- Do we need to order takeout one night?

Write down a few of these logistical realities so
they're clear to both of you.

Side Two: Emotional Intentions

This side is more subtle but just as important. Ask:

- Where is my spouse feeling pressure this
  week?
- How can I show support?
- What small gesture would speak love to
  them?

Maybe your spouse isn't in the mood to cook:
suggest going out. Perhaps they're stressed about
work" plan a quiet night in. Even in "normal" weeks,
emotional connection matters.

The Emotional Weight of Dates

Don't forget special occasions. As one participant
noted: "Mother's Day is next weekend, and two days

later is my wife's birthday. Double whammy!" These events carry emotional significance and deserve intentional planning. But it starts with asking each other questions about their expectations.

Talk about what matters to your partner:

- Do they want a big celebration or something quiet?
- Is this day emotionally loaded or simply another Sunday?

Feeding Ourselves: What Are You Really Consuming?

Next, we'll move from planning to nourishment: what we feed ourselves physically, emotionally, and spiritually. And spoiler alert: food might be a hidden love language you didn't know you had...

1. How well do you and your spouse currently communicate about logistical details in your week, and where could small adjustments prevent unnecessary tension?
2. What emotional needs or pressures might arise this week for either of you, and how can you proactively support one another?
3. How do unspoken expectations like summer plans, holidays, or family visits impact your relationship, and what steps could you take to align them?
4. How might intentionally blocking "protected time" in your schedule improve rest, connection, and peace in your home?
5. How could using a simple tool, like a 3x5 note card for logistical and emotional planning, help you cultivate consistency and clarity in your marriage?

CHAPTER 14

Feeding the Soul, Mind, and Body

Why We Eat - And Why It Matters

Most of us eat for one simple reason: to stay alive. But if you really think about it, the act of eating often serves deeper purposes. We eat to be healthy and strong. We eat because food tastes good and brings us joy. We eat for comfort on cold days - like sipping hot chocolate - and for fun on road trips, at parties, and during movie nights. Food connects us to others. Meals become social moments, like a cruise ship dinner where you sit for hours, talking and laughing with others.

So, if we understand that feeding our bodies serves physical, emotional, and social needs, why wouldn't we apply the same intention to feeding our souls and minds?

Feeding the Soul: Spiritual Nourishment

Just like our bodies, our souls need nourishment. When we don't eat, our physical health deteriorates. And when we neglect our spiritual health, our souls begin to wither. Many people don't realize that spiritual starvation is real. It's just less visible than physical hunger.

So, how do we feed our souls?

The most powerful spiritual nourishment comes from God's Word. Scripture is alive and dynamic.

The same passage read five years apart can hit us entirely differently, depending on where we are in life. That's because the Bible speaks into our current season, no matter what we're walking through. It's God's way of talking to us, offering wisdom, correction, and encouragement.

But Scripture isn't the only way to feed your soul. You can also:

- **Listen to spiritual podcasts or sermons.**
- **Join a community or church group.**
- **Spend time in prayer: not just talking, but also listening.**
- **Sit in silence, giving your soul space to rest and reflect.**
- **Dream, imagine, and plan.** These too are spiritual practices when done with intention and purpose.

Ask yourself: are you feeding your soul, or starving it?

- **Are you spiritually malnourished**, trying to get by without time in the Word or within Biblical community?
- **Are you feeding on junk**, filling your soul with distractions, addictions, or toxic influences?
- **Or are you investing in healthy spiritual practices**, creating intentional rhythms of rest, prayer, and Scripture?

Creating Space for Spiritual Health

The reality is, spiritual habits don't happen by accident. You have to **plan for them**. You have to schedule them the same way you'd schedule a meal or a workout.

For many of us, time is the hardest part. The day starts early, ends late, and is packed with noise and responsibilities. If you don't **carve out space intentionally**, chances are it just won't happen.

That's why couples need to **team up** on this. Maybe your spouse needs a half hour of quiet in the evening to read or pray. Can you take on dinner duty so they can have that time? Or maybe your best moment is early in the morning, before the house wakes up: can you make space for that and support one another's efforts?

Think about it like preparing a big family meal. You don't spend hours cooking just to walk away and leave it sitting on the table. You sit down, enjoy it, and make space for connection. Feeding your soul requires the same level of follow-through: prep, plan, then eat.

Feeding the Mind: Emotional Health

Just as our soul needs spiritual nourishment, our minds need emotional care. Life gets busy, work piles up, and stress builds. When we ignore our emotional needs, things start to unravel. Maybe we snap at our spouse or become irritable with the kids. We feel overwhelmed, exhausted, and emotionally brittle.

So, how do we protect our mental and emotional health?

- **Acknowledge what drains you**. Is it too much work? No time to recharge?
- **Notice patterns**. Are you always more reactive when you're hungry, tired, or overstimulated?
- **Create rhythms of mental rest**. Take walks, journal, talk to someone you trust.

When we're emotionally unhealthy, we don't just hurt ourselves - we hurt the people around us. Emotional health is relational health. If we want strong marriages and families, we have to take care of our minds.

And like everything else in life, this doesn't happen automatically. You have to plan for it. You have to talk about it with your spouse and come up with a game plan. Maybe you need a night out, a therapy session, or even just 15 quiet minutes on the porch after dinner. Whatever it is, **communicate and support each other**.

Knowing Yourself, Knowing Each Other – Emotional Awareness and Strategic Support

When we talk about feeding our emotional health, we can't do that effectively unless we understand *what we actually need.* It sounds simple, but many of us never stop to ask the question:

"What rejuvenates me?"

If you don't know the answer to that question, how could your spouse possibly know?

In our marriage, this has been a journey. I've learned that for Gregg to recharge, he needs downtime and alone time. He is what you might call an extroverted introvert. He loves people, he enjoys parties and being social, but he doesn't get recharged by those things. He gets energized by stepping away – by quiet, solitude, and space to let his thoughts settle. That might mean going for a walk, sitting alone outside, or just reading a book in a quiet room.

Now, I am the opposite. I love people too, but when I'm depleted, I want to *be around people.* I find life and energy in community. So, when I've had a long week, what feels good to me is grabbing coffee with a friend, catching a movie, or jumping into a conversation. That's my version of rest.

We are *wired differently.* And that's okay. What matters is that we know this about each other and that we talk about it.

Questions to Ask Yourself (And Each Other):

1. **What rejuvenates me?**
   - Is it time alone? Time with friends? Reading? Nature?
   - For Gregg, the mountains are a holy place; for me, it's the beach. So we make sure that at least once a year we each spend time in those spaces

2. **What drains me?**
   - For Gregg, it's too much social engagement in a row. Too many evenings in a row of activity, conversation, or pressure can leave him feeling emotionally empty.
   - For me, emotional conflict is particularly draining. I need time after an argument, even if Gregg might feel "fine" five minutes later.

When we name what drains us, we can start to *strategically protect* those margins in our schedule. If we have a hectic week ahead, Gregg might say, "Hey Babe, can we guard Saturday afternoon so I can reset?" And I get it, because we've *talked* about it.

3. **What's my happy place?**
   - This doesn't have to be somewhere exotic or expensive. My couch at night after the kids are asleep is one of mine. It's calm. Familiar. Safe.

- Think of the small and big "happy places" in your life. Where do you breathe better? Think more clearly? Plan to go there, even if it's just once a year.

If you don't know your own answers to these questions, don't rush them. Take time to sit with them, write them down, pray about them, or talk them out with your spouse. If you *do* know your answers, communicate them. Create a culture in your marriage where these emotional needs aren't just acknowledged, they're protected.

Feeding Your Body – Physical Health as an Act of Love

We've talked about soul and emotional health. Now let's talk about your body.

Your body is the *only* one you've got. It's the vessel that carries you through your marriage, your parenting, your career, your ministry, *everything*. So, how we care for it matters. Let's be clear. I'm not a personal trainer or a nutritionist. I'm not here to sell a fitness program. But I do know this: when I'm physically healthier, I have more energy. I'm more available to my kids, more resilient during stressful weeks, more present in my marriage.

"Can I be strong and present for my family at the end of a long day?"

That's the real question.

It's not about having six-pack abs or tracking every calorie. It's about *showing up* with energy, consistency, and presence. Sometimes I think about it this way: if my daughters want to go for a bike ride after dinner, will I have the energy to say yes, or will I crash on the couch because I've neglected my health?

And yes, confidence plays a role. We're not dating anymore, but I still want to look my best for Gregg – not out of vanity, but out of *honor*. He sees me every day. That matters.

So here are a few reflective questions:

- Am I fueling my body well?
- Am I moving in ways that give me strength and energy?
- Am I doing this out of love for myself, my spouse, my family?

Don't overcomplicate it. Just start where you are. Choose one habit. And remember: *physical energy fuels emotional resilience.*

Know Your Why

Let's bring it all together.

Why do you plan?
Why do you pursue physical health?
Why do you care about your emotional bandwidth or your happy places?

If you can't answer that question – what your "why" is – none of this will stick. You'll go back to the same old patterns. The same exhaustion. The same tension in your marriage.

After a major rupture in our marriage years ago, Gregg realized he didn't just need new habits, he needed *clarity*. So he wrote a small book for me called **"My Whys."** He needed me to know what drives him, on the good days and the hard days.

His little book included:

- **Why I follow Christ**
  What He means to Gregg. Why He's central in our marriage. What Gregg believes when no one's watching.
- **Why I love Lize**
  Not just "I love you", but *why*. A list. A reminder. Something he could come back to on the days he felt insecure or frustrated.
- **Why I love our daughters**
  He named what he cherished in each of them. Their personalities. Their quirks. Their worth.
- **Why I run a business**
  It's not just about money. It's about calling, stewardship, providing, and creating space for others to thrive.

That book helped rebuild trust. Not because it was perfect. But because it was *anchored*. And because it gave me a window into his heart.

So, let me challenge you:

- Write your own "Why" book. Even if it's just a page.
- Share it with your spouse.
- Keep it nearby for the hard days.
- Let it drive your decisions, your rhythms, your plans.

An Important Reminder:

You can't lead your marriage well if you're constantly reacting. You need *vision*. Emotional clarity. Physical presence. Spiritual depth.

And all of that flows from your **why**.

Don't wait until things fall apart to figure that out. Start now.

Creating Guilt-Free Space: Why We Do What We Do

Another major piece of our journey has been learning how to create **guilt-free space** for each other.

There was a time when we poured guilt on each other without even realizing it. Sometimes it was subtle, like a sigh when the other person wanted a night out. Other times, it was more overt, like passive-aggressive comments: *"How long are you going to be out?"* or *"I guess I'll be stuck here with the kids again."*

The result? Nobody enjoyed their free time. Guilt hovered over everything.

It took intentional conversations to realize we were living in a cloud of guilt. And once we noticed it, we worked hard to create a new pattern: **freedom, encouragement, and mutual support**. That meant saying:
"Hey, I know poker night fills your cup. Go have a great time."
Or:
"You've had a rough week. Go take a walk, be by yourself. I've got this."

We had to identify what **feeds us** and what **drains us**. What rejuvenates you? What sucks the life out of you? What do you need to feel like yourself again?

Once we could name those things for ourselves and share them with each other, we could begin helping each other live healthier, fuller lives, *without guilt*.

Here are a few conversation starters to help you begin:

- What are your "happy places," big or small?
- What's something you can do in 15 minutes that leaves you feeling refreshed?
- What activities make you feel alive? Which ones make you feel empty?
- Do you feel guilt when you take time for yourself? Why?

Talk honestly about how you both experience guilt and work together to remove it.

Practice Makes Permanent

At first, this kind of intentional planning might feel awkward or overly structured. You might even feel silly, like, *"We love each other, shouldn't we just know this stuff already?"* But love doesn't automatically translate into clarity or communication.

We compared it to our daughter learning volleyball. In her first year, she just had to hit the ball over and over: hundreds, maybe thousands of times. Sometimes it flew sideways or hit the ceiling. But she kept at it. Now, it's second nature to her.

The same thing happens in marriage. It starts off clunky. You try to sit down and talk about your week, and maybe you argue about whether the calendar is shared or not. You try to plan a date night and discover you're on totally different wavelengths. You ask your spouse what rejuvenates them, and they say, *"I don't even know."*

But keep practicing. Just like volleyball for our daughter, what once felt awkward eventually becomes intuitive. Communication deepens. Trust grows. Planning becomes playful. And the guilt begins to dissolve.

A Simple Weekly Challenge

So here's a challenge for the coming month: keep it simple and make it your own:

1. **Have a weekly planning meeting**. This doesn't need to be long, even 15 to 20 minutes is a win. Include three key areas:
   - Logistical (schedules, meals, rides)
   - Emotional (check-in, how are we doing?)
   - Practical (any plans or events we're preparing for)
2. **Plan two date nights this month**. Do it with intention.
   Before the date, ask: *What do we want this night to be?*
   Maybe one of you just wants to laugh and see a movie, while the other is craving deeper conversation. Talk about that in advance, and take turns planning nights based on what the *other* person would love.
3. **Put your long-term planning meeting on the calendar**.
   The meeting doesn't have to happen tomorrow. But look ahead a month or two and schedule a "mini retreat." Whether it's a full day, an overnight, or a few coffee dates: it's powerful to step back and look at the big picture together.

You'll be amazed at how much clarity and connection comes from carving out space to talk about your life *on purpose*. And when you do it with grace instead of guilt, it becomes something you *look forward to*.

Chapter 14 *Reflection Questions:*

1. How intentionally are you feeding your soul, mind, and body on a regular basis, and what areas feel neglected?
2. What specific practices or rhythms help you feel spiritually, emotionally, and physically nourished, and how could you make them more consistent?
3. How well do you understand your own and your spouse's "happy places," drains, and rejuvenation needs, and how could this awareness improve your relationship?
4. Where in your life do guilt or unspoken expectations prevent you from caring for yourself or supporting your spouse, and how can you create guilt-free space?
5. What is your personal "why" for maintaining spiritual, emotional, and physical health, and how can that purpose guide your habits and shared planning with your spouse?

Part 5

FAMILY ROOM

CHAPTER 15

The Heart of the Home

There's a room in nearly every home that represents more than furniture, carpet, or flat-screen TVs. It's the family room, the heart of the house. Just like the physical heart in our bodies, the family room plays a central role in keeping our family life healthy, connected, and alive.

Think of your family room. It may not be the most decorated or the most private space, but it's where people gather. It's the place where laughter echoes, where arguments begin and end, where movie nights happen, where friends sit down for a chat, and where children sprawl across the floor. It's where life pulses.

And just like our physical hearts pump blood throughout our entire body, sustaining every limb and organ, the family room is where emotional, relational, and spiritual lifeblood flows. When the heart of the home is neglected, disconnected, or spiritually dry, everything else suffers.

The Symbolic Heart

The Bible speaks of the heart in profound ways. Proverbs 4:23 says, "Above all else, guard your heart, for everything you do flows from it." The family room is more than a couch and coffee table, it is a symbolic heart. It's where everything flows from in a household.

Just as we measure life by hearing the first heartbeat of a child in the womb, we can often measure the health of a home by the emotional and spiritual rhythm of its family room. Is there laughter? Is there connection? Is there life?

I remember the first time we heard the heartbeat of our first child during a sonogram. It was just a blip on the screen, but it marked life. In the same way, we must pause and ask: what's the heartbeat of our home? Is there evidence of life, connection, and purpose, or has the pulse grown faint?

A Place of Intentional Welcome

Practically speaking, when someone visits your home, where do they go? If it's not the kitchen, it's the family room. It's the room that most often welcomes outsiders. It reflects who you are, what you value, and how you live. Is it inviting? Does it speak of peace? Joy? Love?

As someone who grew up in a military family, I've seen how the heart longs for a place of belonging. Every heartwarming reunion video of a soldier returning home, every hug between a parent and a child: those aren't just emotional moments. They reveal something deeply spiritual: we are made to connect. God designed us for communion. That's why the family room matters.

Three Dimensions of the Heart: Physical, Emotional, and Spiritual

When we talk about "heart," we're speaking in three realms:

- **Physically**, the heart keeps the body alive.
- **Emotionally**, the heart processes our deepest feelings: love, anger, grief, joy.
- **Spiritually**, it's the seat of our connection with God. As children, we are told Jesus lives in our hearts. Even in our childish understanding (and sometimes hilarious interpretations, like my daughter who believed that since God is "in" us, he would love the pizza she eats), that idea of Christ dwelling in us is foundational.

Your family room, in this metaphor, serves each of those three functions too.

Part 1: The Physical Space – Where Life Happens

"It's not just a house: it's where life happens."

Some people think a house is just walls and a roof. But that's like saying a body is just skin and bones. It may be structurally true, but it misses the essence of what a home should be.

The physical space of your home should reflect who you are. And your family room should invite others in. Ask yourself:

- **Is it welcoming?** Could someone stop by and feel like they belong there?
- **Is it organized?** Is the space clear enough to enjoy, to sit in, to connect?
- **Is it intentional?** Do the objects, colors, photos, and decor reflect your values?

Our home is not perfect. We've left Christmas lights out far past the season and had corners cluttered for months. But perfection isn't the goal. Purpose is.

Think about creating not just a room but an experience. Something as intentional and immersive as a trip to Disney. You're not just offering space. You're offering safety, beauty, and connection. That's what the physical heart does for the body: i provides consistent, sustaining energy. What would it look like to let your family room do the same?

Part 2: The Emotional Pulse – How We Relate

Our family rooms should be a relational hub. Is it?

Or is everyone scattered on screens, in separate rooms, behind walls?

A well-used family room brings people together. Not perfectly, not without effort, but intentionally. Create spaces where:

- Families can gather on the couch.
- Conversations can happen naturally.
- Kids can pull out photo albums and remember their stories.

In our home, we've printed annual family yearbooks, full of pictures, memories, and little details. They're on our bookshelf in the family room. Our kids flip through them and remember. That's important. Remembering grounds us. It keeps us rooted in who we are and where we've been.

Are you creating emotional space for your family to connect and remember?

Part 3: The Spiritual Center – Is God at Home Here?

A family room, at its best, is sacred ground.

It may not look like a church pew or a prayer closet, but this is often where God does His most powerful work: in the ordinary. In the messy, joyful, sometimes chaotic family room. This is where spiritual conversations begin. Where Bibles rest on coffee tables. Where a framed verse offers encouragement. Where kids pray before bed. Where guests sense peace.

Ask yourself:

- Are there spiritual markers in our home?
- Would someone sense that Christ is welcome here?

- Does this room reflect our desire to know and serve God?

We don't need to turn our family rooms into sanctuaries, but we do need to invite God into them. He desires to dwell in the heart of our homes just as much as in the hearts of His people.

Important Reminder:

Your family room doesn't need to be Pinterest-perfect to be powerful. It doesn't need matching pillows or the latest renovation trends. But it does need *life*. It needs presence. It needs warmth.

When the heart of the home is alive, the rest of the house thrives.

So step back and listen. Do you hear the heartbeat?

The Heart of Your Home

"By wisdom a house is built, and through understanding it is established; through knowledge its rooms are filled with rare and beautiful treasures." Proverbs 24:3–4

The Physical Space With Purpose

Let's talk about the *why* behind your home. Why do you live where you live? What purpose does your physical space serve?

Gregg and I once lived in a very small apartment, tiny by any standard. But we filled that space with people, laughter, and purpose. We squeezed chairs around a table and crammed in as much community as that space could hold. And it worked, because our *why* was clear: we wanted our home to be a tool for connection, not a display piece.

If you live in a larger home, ask yourself:

- **Can I fill this space with life, or am I just maintaining empty rooms?**
- **Is there someone in need that I could invite in?**
- **Is my home a tool for ministry, hospitality, and generosity?**

And it goes both ways. Maybe you're feeling stretched financially or emotionally by your space. Is it time to downsize? Simplify? Free up resources for something God is calling your family to?

This isn't about guilt or obligation;it's about *intentionality*. Know *why* you're in the house you're in and ask God how to use it with purpose.

Location, Location, Location... With a Mission

A realtor might emphasize proximity to schools or resale value. But what about *missional location*?

Are you planted where you are for a reason? Are you near your church, your community, your people? Are you where your gifts can be used, your family can flourish, and your roots can grow deep?

Or perhaps God is nudging you toward change;something more isolated, more urban, more open to community life. Location isn't just geography;it's strategy. Let your *family mission* shape where you live.

The Emotional Climate of Your Home

Think for a moment: Was there a house you loved going to as a child? A place where the moment you walked in, you felt peace? Safety? Joy?

That atmosphere had little to do with square footage or furniture. It was about *the emotional and spiritual climate.*
I remember friends coming to my parents' home and just wanting to hang out;even when I wasn't there yet! My parents created a home where love was tangible, and everyone felt welcome.

Years later, I heard a powerful testimony from a friend who grew up in an emotionally abusive household. What changed his life? A neighbor's family who consistently invited him in. A mom who didn't hesitate to add a plate at dinner. A home where he felt seen, safe, and valued. It was in that kitchen, over years of dinners, that he met Jesus.

Hospitality isn't just about meals; it's about *ministry.* It's about being willing to create emotional safety in a broken world.

Home Is Not the Building; It's the Belonging

The environment you build will shape your family's memories. Sometimes, it's the smallest things: a blanket on a worn-out couch, the sound of a grandfather clock, a cozy chair that becomes "the spot." These details matter, not because of their expense, but because of the emotion they carry.

As I have mentioned before, since I grew up in a military family, the actual *house* changed many times, but the *feeling* of home stayed the same. Why? Because my parents knew that *home is where your people feel safe and loved.*

1. When you think about your own family room, what emotions or memories come to mind? Does it feel like the "heart" of your home?
2. How does the physical space of your home reflect your values, priorities, and sense of welcome to both family and guests?
3. In what ways can you create or strengthen the emotional connections in your home – through conversation, traditions, or shared experiences?
4. How might you invite God more intentionally into the spiritual center of your home so that His presence can be felt in everyday moments?
5. What changes, big or small, could you make in your home to foster peace, belonging, and purpose for your family and others who enter?

CHAPTER 16

Who Is Your Family, Really?

If someone asked you to describe your family, what would you say?

Most people respond with surface-level details: where they live, what school their kids go to, or what activities they're involved in.

But what if you could answer like this:

"We're a family who loves adventure."
"We're a home who opens our door to others."
"We're intentional about kindness, grace, and shared purpose."

To answer like that, you need clarity on *who you are at the core.* That begins with something most families skip: a **family mission statement.**

Creating Your Family Mission Statement

A mission statement isn't just for businesses or churches. Your family, God's intentional placement of individuals under one roof, has a *mission.* And that mission deserves to be named.

What Is a Family Mission Statement?

It's a unified, intentional expression of:

- What your family is all about
- The kind of life you want to build
- The values and principles you want to live by

"Our family exists to love God, love others, and create a home that reflects grace and belonging."

Your mission can be spiritual, practical, quirky, heartfelt. The point is: it's *yours*. Don't outsource it to a home décor sign from Hobby Lobby.

Why Create One?

Because clarity brings unity. When you're faced with decisions, from vacations to volunteer work to what to say "no" to, you'll have a *why* to come back to.

Don't let life shape your family accidentally. Shape it on purpose.

When Should You Start?

Now. Whether you're newlyweds, in the thick of raising toddlers, guiding teens, or empty nesters, your family has a mission worth articulating.

Even if you think, *"My kids are too young,"* bring them in anyway. They may say silly things, but that process teaches them: *We are a team. We are intentional. We have purpose.*

And if you're in a new phase – kids grown, house quieter than it used to be – don't skip this. Your mission has just entered a new season.

Reflect and Create

Take some time this week to sit down with your spouse or your whole family and ask:

- What do we want to be known for?
- What kind of atmosphere do we want people to feel in our home?
- What values do we want to guide our decisions?
- How do we want to use our space?
- What legacy do we want to leave?

Write it down. Frame it if you want. But most of all – *live it.*

Family Challenge:
Write your family mission statement together this week.
Include every voice, even the littlest ones. Keep it simple, memorable, and reflective of who God is calling you to be.

Creating a Family Mission Statement

"Without this vision, kids can be swept along with the flow of society's values and trends. It's simply living out the scripts that have been given to you. In fact, it's really not living at all. It's being lived."
– Stephen Covey

A Vision That Anchors the Soul of the Family

As children grow, so do their questions: *Who am I? Where do I belong? What is this home all about?* These questions become louder during the teenage years and even more defining when they leave home to start their own families. If we don't guide them intentionally, society will. Culture, trends, and peer pressure will take the driver's seat and define their values for them.

Every child longs to belong. If we as parents don't establish a meaningful place of identity, our children will look for that belonging elsewhere – often in shallow waters: social media, material success, popularity, or performance. But what if we, as a family, offered something more grounded, more sacred: a clearly articulated family mission?

When you create a shared family mission, you're not just hanging words on a wall. You're carving out a foundation of identity and purpose. You are defining who you are, where you're going, and why your family exists. That clarity becomes an anchor, especially in seasons of chaos, transition, or testing.

Why a Shared Family Vision Matters

A thoughtfully crafted family mission statement becomes a compass, helping everyone from toddlers to teens to parents navigate life with shared understanding. It's not about perfection. It's about connection, direction, and values lived out daily.

Here's what a shared family vision can do:

- **Guide parenting decisions:** Instead of reacting emotionally or inconsistently, you now have a shared framework to reflect back on.
- **Foster ownership and buy-in:** When kids help build the mission, they're more likely to live it out.
- **Create emotional and spiritual unity:** Your family becomes a team, pulling in the same direction with shared purpose.
- **Develop accountability and identity:** When disagreements arise, you have a central standard to return to: *Is this in line with who we say we are?*
- **Distinguish your home from the world's noise:** In a world full of options, you've chosen intentionality.

I remember the first time we made "salmon fish pockets" with the kids. If I had just served it, I would've gotten complaints about the "green stuff" (pesto) on top of the fish. But instead, I invited them into the process. One child made a salad, another seasoned the fish and added the toppings, and another set the table. By the time we sat down, they couldn't wait to eat. Why? Because they owned it. The same principle applies to your mission statement: when kids help shape it, they'll be proud to live it.

Practical Steps to Build a Family Mission Statement

This isn't a one-night assignment. It's a process. Take your time, allow conversation, and most importantly, make it fun and memorable.

1. Schedule a Family Meeting

Choose a relaxed time when everyone is emotionally available – maybe over dinner, a Saturday morning brunch, or even during a family retreat. If you have little ones, keep it short and sweet, and break the process into multiple gatherings.

Everyone gets a say. Yes, even the three-year-old who thinks the family should be about pizza and playgrounds.

2. Use Guiding Questions

If you need help starting the conversation, use a worksheet like the "Family Questions" handout included in this book. Ask things like:

- What is the purpose of our family?
- What kind of atmosphere do we want in our home?
- What values matter most to us?
- What do we want others to feel when they visit our home?

Write everything down. Words. Phrases. Feelings. Even scribbles from toddlers.

3. Define Your Core Values

Create a list of the values that make your family unique. Don't try to impress others. This is for *you*. Be honest about what resonates.

Here are a few starters:

- Faith
- Integrity
- Hospitality
- Humor
- Learning
- Health
- Service
- Compassion

Whittle the list down to 5–10 that feel most foundational.

4. Craft Meaningful Phrases

Turn those values into simple statements or phrases. You can pull from movies, Scripture, family sayings, or your own words.

Examples:

- "We keep moving forward." (from *Meet the Robinsons*)
- "In this home, grace comes first."
- "We laugh loud, forgive fast, and love big."

Don't worry about style. Just focus on heart.

5. Consolidate into 10 or Fewer Ideas

If you find yourself with pages of content, that's great! Now, simplify. Combine similar ideas into unified statements. Aim for clarity without losing meaning.

6. Write the Statement

Keep it under 100 words, if possible. Make sure every person feels represented. Take your time. It may take days or weeks. That's okay.

7. Display It

Put your family mission where it can be seen often: on a canvas, a framed print, painted wood, or even on the fridge. This makes it real. Kids read what they see, and when it becomes part of the environment, it becomes part of their thinking.

In our home, we've placed mission words and values along the stairwell, words like "joy," "family," "grace," and "laughter." In our kitchen, a simple sign reads: *This kitchen is made for dancing*. And yes, we dance there often.

8. Live It. Use It. Review It.

Your family will grow and change, so revisit your mission every couple of years. Update it when new seasons begin, when kids grow, when you become empty nesters, or when you feel like your rhythm needs resetting.

Sample Mission Statements

Here are a few real-life examples to inspire your own:

Example 1:

Love the Lord above all else. Always be honest. Count your blessings. Bear one another's burdens. Forgive and forget. Be kind and tenderhearted. Keep your promises. Support one another. Treat others as you want to be treated. Love deeply from the heart.

Example 2:

Our mission as a family is to love each other and love our neighbor. We commit to be there for each other, work as a team, and face challenges together. We aim to be caring, helpful, encouraging, and loyal. We serve with humility and never give up on one another.

Example 3:

In this family, we laugh, play, tell the truth, work hard, and show respect. We make mistakes and say "I'm sorry." We do hugs, offer grace, and always stick together. Our home is a safe place where everyone belongs.

"Where there is no vision, the people perish."

Proverbs 29:18

Chapter 16 *Reflection Questions*:

1. How would you currently describe the identity and purpose of your family, and what would you like it to become?
2. In what ways could creating a family mission statement help bring clarity, unity, and direction to your family's decisions and daily life?
3. What core values do you want to define your family culture, and how can you intentionally communicate and live them out?
4. How might including every family member, even young children, in the mission statement process impact their sense of belonging and purpose?
5. Looking ahead, what legacy do you want your family to leave for future generations, and how can a mission statement help shape that legacy?

CHAPTER 17

Creating the Emotional Atmosphere of Your Home

When we think of our homes, most of us imagine walls, furniture, rooms filled with life, activity, and hopefully, peace. But beyond the physical, every home carries an invisible atmosphere – a mood, a tone, an emotional temperature that can either soothe the soul or stir up anxiety. And whether we realize it or not, we are the ones setting that atmosphere.

We've spent time talking about the physical space of your home: how it looks, how it functions, how it can become more inviting. But there's another side: **the emotional space**, and it matters just as much. Maybe even more.

You and I create the emotional tone of our homes. It's not just what's hanging on the walls or stacked in the garage. It's what people feel when they walk through the front door. It's the way we carry our stress, our love, our energy, our communication. And let's be honest, that's often easier said than done.

For some of you, this is a particularly hard season to create emotional warmth. You may be dealing with marriage challenges, strained family dynamics, financial stress, or grief. These burdens are real, and they absolutely affect the atmosphere of a home. If you're feeling stuck or overwhelmed, please know this: **you're not alone**, and it's okay to reach out for help. This is not about being perfect. It's about being intentional.

Is Your Home a Place of Peace?

Ask yourself: *When you or someone else steps into your home, what do they feel?*

Do they feel tension? Stress? A sense of walking into the middle of an argument or unspoken frustration? Or do they feel safety, laughter, rest, and warmth?

Sometimes we don't even realize what we're broadcasting emotionally. But others can feel it. You can feel it. You walk into the family room and something is *off*. Or maybe, when you pull into the driveway, you sit in the car a little longer just to avoid stepping into it.

This isn't just emotional. It can be physical too. Maybe it's cluttered spaces, unfinished projects, or physical disorganization that weighs on you the moment you walk in. That pile of Christmas decorations still in the garage in June? It's more than an eyesore. It can be a symbol of lingering stress or mental overwhelm.

Whether physical or emotional, this tension matters. And you have the power to change it.

What Do Others Feel When *You* Come Home?

It's not just about how we feel walking into the house. It's also about how others feel when we arrive.

Think about this: *when you come home, does the emotional atmosphere rise or fall?*

Do you walk in with joy, laughter, hugs, and warmth? Or are you dragging in the stress of your day, your worries, or your irritability? Are you quick to greet your spouse or children with love...or silence?

Even if you've had a tough day, even if you're not okay, you can still choose to greet your family with some form of grace. A smile. A simple, "Hey, it's good to see you." A moment of softness can change the whole evening.

You have the power to set the tone the moment you walk through the door.

Define What "Home" Means to You

What does "home" mean to you? Think back to your childhood. Was it a place of comfort or chaos? Warmth or fear? Whatever it was, you have the chance now to define your home with fresh meaning.

Is home a place of safety? Of laughter? Of truth? Of refuge? Of being known?

Take time to reflect and even write it out. If you don't define what "home" means to you, how can your spouse or children live into that vision with you?

And remember, **home is more than a place**. It's a feeling. A culture. A message we send every day through our words, actions, routines, and presence.

Is Your Home a Safe Place?

Not just physically, but emotionally?

Can your family be themselves there?
Can they talk without fear of being judged?
Can they breathe?

A safe home is where we can let down our guards. It's where we can find renewal. It's not just a house. It's an emotional and spiritual haven. You don't have to be wealthy or perfectly organized to build that. You just have to choose to have love, grace, and connection form the foundation.

A Family Story: Home in a Hotel Room

Some dear friends of ours live in California. During a season of devastating wildfires, they found themselves in a situation where both the home they were renting and the one they were building were under threat. They evacuated, packed their family into a hotel, and waited.

They didn't know if either house would survive. All their possessions were at risk.

But here's what they held onto: their family was together. They decided to create peace and warmth even in that hotel room. Five kids, no space, and piles of uncertainty, but still, laughter. Still, prayer. Still, love.

Because home isn't a structure. It's a spirit. And they carried that spirit with them.

You Have the Power to Change the Atmosphere

If your home isn't what you want it to be, *don't give up*. You have choices. You have a vision. You have the ability to wake up each day and shift one small thing.

Maybe today it's choosing not to raise your voice. Maybe it's lighting a candle and playing soft music while the family gathers.
Maybe it's greeting your spouse at the door with a kiss, no matter how tired you feel.

You are a thermostat, not a thermometer. You don't just read the emotional temperature; you set it.

A Word from Hoda and Maria

In a touching moment from the *Today Show*, Hoda Kotb and Maria Shriver shared their thoughts on home:

"I can't change everything going on in the world, but I can make it peaceful here... I want it to feel soft when they come home. I might not be able to fix everything, but I can do this."

They reminded us that people crave comfort, connection, and invitation. They spoke of candles, blankets, food, simple things that communicate love. But it goes deeper.

Maria said:

"Home starts here."
(She pointed to her heart.)
"If you're at peace because you're loving, happy, inviting, your home will be that."

Let that sink in.

Home isn't just where you live; it's how you live with the people God has given you. Create it with love. Build it with peace. Fill it with grace.

Even if the walls fall down, you'll still have each other.

And that, my friend, is home.

Creating a Home of Peace and Purpose

A couple came to us struggling with something that might seem minor to outsiders, but anyone in a marriage knows it's often the small, repetitive pain points that cause the deepest disconnect.

Each evening, when the garage door opened, instead of a sense of anticipation or welcome, a feeling of dread crept in. The spouse's arrival felt more like an interruption than a return. We worked with this couple and revisited concepts we'd covered in earlier sessions. One practical tool we offered was deceptively simple: index cards.

We asked them to write out what they *wanted* from that transition moment. Just a few words: "When you walk through this door, I want a hug." Not "when you walk in, I need you to stop being grumpy" or "don't go straight to the TV," but a vision of connection. Something as small as a 20-second hug, not requiring any words or grand gestures, could reshape the climate of their home.

By the end of the week, they called with joy in their voices. The shift was undeniable. When she heard the garage door open, her heart lifted in anticipation. Something so small, his simple decision to initiate that hug, created a chain reaction of emotional safety and welcome.

It's rarely the grand gestures that heal relationships or transform homes. It's small acts, intentionally repeated, that change everything.

The Power of Words: Reshaping Atmosphere

In one particularly difficult season of our marriage, I stumbled across an article about the words we use and the environments they create. It hit me hard. My go-to word was "quickly."

"Quickly, put your shoes on."

"Quickly, we need to leave."

"Quickly eat, quickly, quickly..."

It was constant. And though I hadn't realized it, my home was becoming a space of pressure and hurriedness. Gregg gently confronted me one day and said, "Our home doesn't feel peaceful. It feels frantic."

That stung. But he was right.

I didn't have to change who I was. I just had to become intentional with my words. It took discipline. I had to slow down my speech and be present. "Let's sit down and put our shoes on together," I'd say. I even practiced inserting the word "quietly" where "quickly" used to be. The transformation in our household atmosphere was astonishing.

Our words create our world.

The Peaceful Home Checklist

We started compiling simple, practical actions that contribute to the emotional and spiritual tone of a home. Here's what we came up with – a checklist for cultivating a peaceful, joyful, God-honoring home:

1. Speak Kindly
Your tone sets the emotional temperature. Choose gentle words. Avoid repeated negativity like "I'm tired" or "This is too much." It affects everyone.

2. Gather Regularly
Have meals together. Create sacred time to talk, laugh, eat, and connect, whether it's with your

spouse, kids, close friends, and/or community group.

3. Laugh Easily

Play, joke, let go. Create an atmosphere where humor and lightness are welcome. It's okay to laugh at yourself.

4. Work with a Cheerful Attitude

The chores never end. But how we approach them shapes the home's spirit. Choose gratitude while folding the laundry or vacuuming the stairs.

5. Give Generously

Your home is not just for you. Let go of the fear of mess or broken things. Invite people in, open your table, and share your space.

6. Forgive Quickly

Grudges are heavy and suffocating. Don't let resentment linger. Extend grace freely and often.

7. Hug a Lot

Physical connection builds emotional safety. Create a home where hugs are frequent, expected, and comforting.

8. Pray Daily

Let God be central. Speak to Him together. Acknowledge His presence in your meals, your conflicts, your laughter, and your plans.

9. Cheer Each Other On

Be your spouse's and your children's biggest fan. Make your home the most affirming space in their lives.

10. Love Genuinely

Understand and express love in the way your people best receive it. Study them. Listen. Invest.

11. Have Fun

Play music. Dance. Host game nights. Create joy. Make your home a place your family *wants* to come back to.

12. Create Memories

You don't need a big budget to make unforgettable moments. Build your family's legacy through intentional time, rituals, and shared experiences.

Becoming a Memory Maker

I am a HUGE advocate of creating traditions and memories. As a child my parents always woke us up on our birthdays with breakfast in bed, singing "happy birthday" and giving us our gifts. I remember, as a child, laying in my bed anticipating the family walking in. It was such a great feeling!

So, I continued that tradition in my own family, and we still do this today (even with my kids who are high school and college). On birthdays, we all pile into the room and sing loudly, off-key, and joyfully, and we serve breakfast in bed. Our kids anticipate this with wide-eyed excitement. It's not about the presents. It's about *being seen* and celebrated.

Memories don't cost much. But they do cost *intentionality*.

You can:

- Take a weekly bike ride.
- Make waffles every Saturday morning.
- Explore local parks or waterfalls.
- Share stories over candlelit dinners.

You're not just passing time. You're building a foundation your children will stand on when life shakes them. You're shaping the way they'll one day build their own homes.

What Kind of House Are You Building?

I love playing Miranda Lambert's *"The House That Built Me."* It's a song about returning home, not just to a building but to the place where identity was formed, where healing is found, and where life makes sense.

That's what a home can be.

Not perfect. Not flawless. But intentional. Peaceful. Welcoming.

Ask yourself:

- Would my children want to return here to heal?
- Am I building a home they'll remember with warmth and gratitude?
- Am I building *a house that builds them*?

You don't need perfection. You need purpose.

Let's become memory-makers, peace-speakers, and builders of healing homes. Let's make home the place we, and those we love, always want to come back to.

1. When someone walks into your home, what emotional "temperature" do they feel? Does it reflect the environment you want to create?
2. How do your words, tone, and daily habits influence the emotional and spiritual climate of your home?
3. What memories or traditions from your own childhood shaped your view of "home," and how are you continuing, or changing, that legacy in your family today?
4. In what ways could small, intentional actions (like a warm greeting, laughter, or prayer) transform the atmosphere of your home this week?
5. If your children were to describe the emotional environment of your home in one sentence, what do you hope they would say;and what steps can you take to make that a reality?

Part 6

CHILDREN'S BEDROOM

CHAPTER 18

The Beautiful Mess of Parenting

I get to share the discussion of this "room" with one of my dearest friends, and that's always a joy. Summer and I have been friends for several years now, ever since my family moved to Florida. Our kids go to school together, and we attempt (key word: attempt) to walk three miles together a few times a week. Really, it's more of a walking chat session, which often ends in smoothies and sometimes terrible movies, but we love it. It's been a gift to do life together in the mess and fun of everyday parenting.

More than a friend, I have deep respect for Summer. Her passion for families, for children, and for walking alongside them in times of crisis is something to behold. She brings wisdom to the table without overwhelming you. Her advice is clear, practical, and rooted in experience and compassion. She is a licensed mental health counselor, a specialist in working with children and families, and a board member of Liz's Legacy, a local foundation that helps children access mental health counseling when their families can't afford it.

So in this "room" of your house, I get the opportunity to let Summer share her wisdom with you, and I'm thrilled because I know you're going to walk away with truth, encouragement, and tools that will serve you, whether you're parenting a newborn or relating to adult children, whether you're a parent by choice, by chance, or through your relationships with nieces, nephews, godchildren, or neighbors. Every single one of us has been touched by the life of a child, and every one of us has the power to touch a child's life in return. Our relationships are not separate boxes; they are all connected. They grow together, break together, and heal together.

So with no further ado, I'll hand it over to Summer for the remainder of this Chapter and Chapter 19! Thanks, Summer, for your wisdom!

From Fear to Flourishing

I'm so grateful for the way Lize lives her life out loud – vulnerable, honest, real. She gives people permission to say, "We're struggling too".

One reason I love working with Lize is that she is so fun! She prioritizes fun and joy in her family life, and our family has benefitted so much from being a part of the fun she creates. This is also a reason I love working with children - it's *really* fun. Fun, joy, and play are some of the best elements of a thriving, healthy family life. It's so important that we want to make sure this is the starting point for these chapters.

Here are a few prompts you can use to generate a quick, playful moment. These moments diffuse stress and set the tone for the evening when everyone is home from work and school and transitioning into the remainder of the day.

1) Teach me a new dance move you've learned recently.
2) Play me a song you are loving right now.
3) If you could choose one fun thing to do today, what would it be?
4) Teach me a new slang word I wouldn't know.

From Teenage Mom to Family Counselor

So first, a little bit about me - I was a teenage parent: clueless, self-absorbed, and completely unaware of how to attune to the needs of my child. God has brought me a long way from there.

Today, I'm a licensed counselor, a speaker, a mom of three (ages 29, 18, and 14), a grandmother, and a wife to my husband, Jay.

Jay and I started our parenting journey at 19 and 17. Back then, we never could've imagined the family we have now. And while I'm still growing, the difference between the parent I was then and who I am today is nothing short of transformation.

Parenting has been the greatest teacher of my life. God has used it to stretch me in ways I could've never predicted, to grow me into someone more patient, more compassionate, and more humble.

Four Core Truths About Parenting

1. There's No Such Thing as a Perfect Parent

Let's just release that pressure right now. It doesn't exist. And it's not the goal. If I sat here and claimed to be the perfect parent with perfect kids, most of you would laugh, and rightly so. Parenting is a beautiful **mess**. If you've ever tiptoed into your child's room at night and just stared at their peaceful face, you know that awe and wonder. You back out slowly... and then immediately step on a LEGO and get yanked right back to reality.

Parenting is the ebb and flow of beauty and frustration. And when you can see the beauty even in the mess, that's growth.

2. Parenting Grows Us

The world tells us we're already grown up, that it's the child who's here to be molded. But what if it's not just them who's being shaped?

What if you are growing too?

When your first child is born, a **parent** is also born. Parenting is a developmental process. And God uses it to refine us – sometimes painfully, often beautifully – into people who better reflect His heart.

3. Parenting Is Not a Subject to Master

It's not a skillset to conquer or a checklist to complete. Parenting is a relationship, an ever-evolving, holy connection between you and your child, and between you and your spouse.

It changes with every season. Just when you think you've figured toddlers out, your children become tweens. Just when you master one kid's rhythm, the next one comes along with a totally different beat.

4. Parenting Is Less About What You Do and More About Who You Are

You bring your whole self to your relationship with your child: your beliefs, your trauma, your faith, your personality. The same is true for your spouse. That's why no parenting book fits everyone perfectly. Every parent-child relationship is unique, just like you.

Parenting as Spiritual Formation

What we'll talk about in these next few chapters isn't "how to parent right." We're not here to teach you techniques to produce perfectly behaved kids. Instead, we want to explore how **God uses parenting to form us** - to heal us and to grow us.

God is the perfect Father. And in parenting, He reveals His heart to us – His patience, His mercy, His justice, His love.

As we pursue intimacy with God, just like in our marriages, we find the source of joy, peace, and resilience for the journey of raising children.

Whether you're a parent by biology, adoption, fostering, or relationship, this journey matters. Not just for the next generation, but for **who we are becoming** in the process.

So where do we begin? **Parent Together with God at the Center**

Becoming One in the Parenting Journey

Let's start with a reminder that may sound obvious but is often overlooked: parenting is not just about children. It's also deeply about **marriage**. As a husband and wife, you each bring into the relationship the parenting styles and experiences of your upbringing. Your parents likely did some things well and other things not so well. When two people come together in marriage, they're not just forming a new relationship, they're also forming a new family culture. That includes making decisions about **how to parent**.

This process can be both beautiful and messy. And it's essential to remember: **do not try to figure out how to parent in front of your children**.

We've all been there. The child asks to do something, and one parent immediately says no. Then the other parent chimes in, "Wait, why not? That doesn't seem like a big deal" and suddenly, you're having a debate in front of your kids. It's confusing for them, and it erodes the sense of unity that children need to feel secure.

What's better? Step aside. Take it offline. Revisit the conversation when it's just the two of you. As we often say, **pre-plan your parenting**. Sit down without the kids around and discuss your values, your boundaries, and your "why."

Define, define, define.

Define your discipline approach. Define your goals. Define your expectations.

The more you clarify your parenting philosophy together, the fewer power struggles and confusion you'll have, both between each other and with your children.

And remember: this applies at every stage of parenting. Whether you have toddlers or adult children, parenting evolves. Even in our forties, my siblings and I still see our parents navigate how to relate to us, and they still talk through those decisions privately. The goal is not to control your children but to grow together as parents with wisdom and unity.

Chapter 18 *Reflection Questions*:

1. How has parenting (or your relationships with children in your life) shaped and grown you personally, emotionally, or spiritually?
2. What areas of your parenting or family culture feel messy right now, and how might you begin to see beauty or growth within that mess?
3. How do you and your spouse (or co-parent) work together to create unity in your parenting decisions? What could improve that sense of teamwork?
4. Which part of your parenting approach reflects your own upbringing, and are there things you want to keep, change, or release from that influence?
5. How might viewing parenting as a spiritual formation journey, rather than a skill to master, shift the way you approach challenges with your children?

CHAPTER 19

The Core Question of Every Heart

At the heart of parenting is the heart of the gospel. As human beings, we all long to know:

Am I loved?

Even if I mess up, am I still loved?

This is the heartbeat of the message we want our children to receive. This is what they are desperately asking – sometimes through words, sometimes through behavior. And the answer from our heavenly Father is always: **Yes. You are loved. Even when you mess up.**

If we want to answer our children with that same love and grace, we must begin with **our own intimacy with God**.

"We love because He first loved us." – *1 John 4:19*

Our spiritual life isn't about trying harder to be righteous parents. It's about going deeper into intimacy with God. Years ago, our pastor said something that stayed with me:

"Don't work at righteousness, work at intimacy with God."

That simple phrase transformed my perspective. I realized I didn't need to **strive** to be patient, gentle, or peaceful. Instead, I needed to **abide**. To rest in God. To talk with Him. To read His Word. To worship. To make space for silence, reflection, and prayer.

From that intimacy, the fruits of the Spirit naturally grow: love, joy, peace, patience, kindness, goodness, faithfulness, gentleness, and self-control. These are not traits we manufacture. They are fruits of a life rooted in God.

Knowing God the Way You Know Your Children

We know our children because we spend time with them. We see their habits, we hear the tone in their voices, we notice the subtle shifts in their moods. Even when they're grown, we can pick up on how they're doing with just a glance or a sentence.

So how do we expect to know God, or reflect Him, if we're not spending time with Him?

You cannot expect to respond to your spouse or your children with godly wisdom and grace if you haven't been with the One who gives it. Parenting in the way God calls us to is impossible without **Him**. Not without rules. Not without a book. Without **Him.**

And the truth is: God already knows you. He's inviting you to know Him more deeply.

That doesn't mean hours of isolated Bible study while the house is falling apart. It means weaving God into the rhythms of your life:

- Reading a verse while drinking your morning coffee

- Praying while driving your kids to school

- Listening to worship music while folding laundry

- Having Scripture visible in your home

- Thanking God out loud when something small goes well

- Asking for His help out loud when it doesn't

Let your intimacy with God be **visible** to your children. If you want to raise children who rely on God, **show them what that looks like.** Let them see you reach for your Bible. Let them hear you pray. Let them know that God is not a theory or a Sunday experience; He is your life.

Living What You Want to Teach

At the end of the day, your kids aren't just listening to what you say. They are **watching who you are**.

- Do they see you trusting God when things are hard?

- Do they hear kindness in your voice?

- Do they notice you forgiving quickly?

- Do they watch you seek wisdom before reacting?

We all want our kids to grow up with a strong faith. But that starts not with them but with us. Our homes become a reflection of what we truly prioritize. If we want God to be first in their lives, He must be first in ours.

So today, take this to heart: **Don't work at parenting. Work at intimacy with God.**

Because when your life is rooted in Him, everything else, including parenting, flows from that place of grace, peace, and power.

The Power of Presence

There is no greater joy than being in our Father's presence and feeling His loving and protective gaze. In that sacred space, we know who we are – we are deeply loved, fully accepted, and seen. And as parents, we have the incredible privilege of sharing a reflection of that experience with our children.

In this chapter, we'll explore three transformational ways to experience this love:

1. **Loving through Connection**

2. **Joining in Play**

3. **Restoring After Disconnection**

Each is a pathway to deeper relationships, not just between parent and child, but between us and God.

1. Loving Through Connection

"You make known to me the path of life; in your presence there is fullness of joy; at your right hand are pleasures forevermore."   Psalm 16:11 (ESV)

This verse invites us to linger in God's presence, to soak in the joy and love He gives so freely. That same presence becomes our model for parenting. When we offer our full attention to our children without multitasking, judgment, or distraction, we mirror God's unwavering gaze.

Dr. Curt Thompson, a trusted voice in spiritual and emotional health, once said:

"You are goodness and beauty."

Not "you act good," or "you look beautiful," but "you are" intrinsically and irrevocably.

When we slow down enough to be truly present with our children, we begin to see this goodness and beauty in them too. It shows up in their humor, their play, even in their mistakes and messiness. And when we love them right there, in that imperfect moment, we're reflecting the very heart of God.

A Parent's Real-Life Chaos... and Pause

Let's be honest: our daily lives are filled with interruptions.

Hold on, I have a text...

You're supposed to do your homework!

The dryer's buzzing...

Oh no, the water's boiling over!

The boss is calling.

The soccer game started five minutes ago...

Everybody in the car!

Life is loud. Parenting is chaotic.

But in the middle of it all, God invites us to pause.

Be still. Breathe. You are in the presence of the living God.

Now, imagine turning to your child and saying:

"Just for the next 15 minutes, it's going to be just you and me.
No distractions. You get to pick what we do. Let's go."

Can you picture the delight on their face?

This kind of focused attention, simple and sacred, is more powerful than we realize. Five to fifteen minutes, a few times a week, can shape a child's heart more deeply than hours of distracted time.

2. Joining in Play

Young children thrive in play. It's their language, their world. When we follow their lead, we enter that world. In therapy, this approach is often used to build trust and safety with a child. But it's just as effective at home.

This isn't the time to teach or correct. It's not a moment for instruction or fixing. It's simply a time to "be with" our children as they are.

Let them choose the activity. Match their rhythm. Follow their curiosity. Say yes to the pace that feels too slow and resist the itch to redirect.

You might feel bored. That's okay. Stay anyway.

This is where connection is born, not in the grand gestures, but in the mundane moments of shared presence. As they lead the play, we give the gift of being fully with them, with no agenda, no judgment, just love.

3. Restoring Connection

But what about when things go wrong?

Parenting is full of missteps. Harsh words. Short tempers. Moments we regret.

Here's the good news: God never abandons us in our mess. Even when we make irreversible mistakes, His love remains.

That's the model we follow as parents. When connection breaks down, we can come alongside our children to repair it. We can pray together. Apologize. Cry. Laugh again. Try again.

Because grace is more powerful than perfection.

Parenting Teens: Listening with Grace

Now, teenagers don't usually want to sit on the floor and play Thomas the Train (although if they do, lean in!). With teens, connection looks different, but it's just as necessary.

Here's the picture: You arrive, ready to connect. You've spent time with God. Your heart is open. Your metaphorical pitcher is full of clean water, ready to pour into your teen's life.

But they show up holding their own pitcher, full of dirty water.

They're grumpy. Dismissive. Maybe even rude.

This is not a rejection of you. It's a reflection of their inner chaos.

Teenagers are still developing - literally. Neurologically, their brains are unfinished. Their peer groups are their world, and they're caught between family connection and social independence.

When they pour out their "dirty water," they're offering you the chance to be a safe place. A holding space. Not to fix, but to listen.

"Tell me about your day."
"I'm here."
"You don't have to clean it up first."

This kind of listening builds trust. It tells them, "You matter. Right now. As you are."

Why Connection Matters

When we give this gift of focused connection, even briefly, it builds something lasting. Here's what it creates in our children:

- **They feel seen and heard.** They learn that they are accepted as they are.

- **They grow more receptive.** When correction is needed, they're more likely to listen.

- **They become more cooperative.** Our relational investment softens resistance.

- **Their self-worth increases.** They internalize the truth: "I am lovable. I matter."

Final Thoughts

We're all busy. Life doesn't stop. But these moments of connection don't require hours. They require presence.

So this week, pause. Sit. Look into your child's eyes. Let them lead. Just be there.

Because when we connect like this, we're not just building better relationships – we're echoing the very heart of God.

Chapter 19 *Reflection Questions*:

1. When you consider the core question "Am I loved?" how do you communicate to your children, through words and actions, that they are deeply loved, even when they make mistakes?
2. In what ways can you create more space in your daily life to deepen your intimacy with God so that His love naturally flows into your parenting?
3. How often do your children see you practicing your faith in real, everyday ways such as praying, reading Scripture, or thanking God out loud?
4. What simple, distraction-free moments of connection can you intentionally create this week to make your child feel seen, heard, and valued?
5. How do you typically respond when connection with your child is broken, and what steps can you take to bring grace and restoration into those moments?

CHAPTER 20

Creating a Safe Harbor: Parenting with Connection and Consistency

The Power of Connection

Connection greases the wheels of cooperation.

It's true in marriage, in teams, and especially in parenting. When your child feels emotionally connected to you, they are more ready to respond positively. What some might call "first-time obedience" often flows not from fear or discipline alone, but from relationships.

Beyond cooperation, connection actually grows healthy brains. Thanks to the advancements in brain imaging technology over the past two decades, we now know that relationships don't only influence behavior but literally shape the architecture of the brain. Neural pathways form. Brain cells grow. Emotional resilience strengthens.

When we connect with our children, we give them more than affection – we give them the building blocks for social, emotional, and cognitive development. That connection answers the deepest questions of the human heart:

Am I loved? Am I safe? Am I still valuable, even if I mess up?

When you create a relationship in which your child can confidently say "yes" to those questions, you're building more than behavior, you're building wholeness.

Five Keys to Creating a Safe Space

Connection isn't just about closeness; it's about safety. To truly thrive, our kids need to feel secure emotionally, not just physically. Here are five ways to create that kind of safe space:

1. Don't Shame. Listen with Judgment-Free Eyes

We've worked with many families in difficult seasons, some navigating broken marriages, high stress, or even separation. Parenting in the middle of emotional chaos is deeply challenging. But even in those moments, your calling doesn't change: you are still the safest place on earth for your child.

One of the most damaging habits we fall into as parents is unintentionally shaming our children. This especially becomes tempting when emotions run high or when we feel pressure to correct a child in front of others.

Think of a moment at a theme park or a shopping mall where you've likely witnessed a parent yelling at their child in public. The child's body is shrinking with embarrassment. Their ears aren't hearing instruction; their brain is flooded with shame. They aren't thinking, *What can I learn?* They're thinking, *Who is watching me fail?*

Imagine this: you're at a dinner party with friends, and your spouse reprimands you loudly in front of everyone. How would you feel? Small? Exposed? Hurt? Now remember – your children feel the same. They may not have adult vocabulary, but they carry the same emotional wiring.

So ask yourself: Would I speak to my friend this way? Would I want to be corrected like this?

Discipline and guidance are essential, but the delivery matters. Always offer correction in a safe, private environment that preserves dignity, not in ways that publicly embarrass or isolate.

2. Make Yourself Available

We live in a world of constant contact. Phones buzz. Emails ping. Group chats hum.

Ironically, the more connected we are to the world, the more disconnected we can become from the people who matter most, especially our kids.

Your child may not say it out loud, but they're asking:

Am I more important than your inbox? Than your church committee? Than your social media?

My own father modeled this powerfully. Despite a high-demand military career, often in foreign countries, intense meetings, and even combat zones, he always took our calls. He might have answered and said, "I'm in a meeting. Is this urgent?" but we always knew he would answer.

That simple act sent a powerful message: *You matter to me. I'm available.*

Today, I see the ripple effect of his availability in my own children. My niece recently said, "I know Grandad's number by heart; he always answers." That's the legacy of availability: security.

Being present doesn't mean being perfect or always available at the exact moment. But it does mean creating a culture where your family knows they are prioritized. When your child calls, answer. When they reach out, respond. Even if it's just a quick "I'm proud of you" or "Let's talk when I get home." These moments will form a lasting impression.

3. Be Consistent and United

Your children need stability, and one of the most important ways to provide it is through unity in your marriage. If your child senses that they can divide and conquer, asking one parent after the other until they get the answer they want, you're not only creating confusion but insecurity.

Consistency for your children begins with your relationship as husband and wife. Next to your relationship with God, your marriage is your most important priority. When that relationship is strong, it provides a foundation of peace and security for your children.

Let your kids see you as a team. Even when it annoys them, even when they roll their eyes at your united front, it communicates: *We are stable. We are safe. We are on the same side.*

Children may push boundaries, but what they truly crave is consistency. A team approach;where Mom and Dad are in sync;creates an environment of trust.

4. Set Boundaries that Protect

Imagine this: a van from the local prison pulls up to your home with a group of dangerous strangers inside. Would you leave your doors open? Would you let them wander inside and spend time in your living room?

Of course not.

But every day, many of us allow harmful influences into our homes without a second thought, through screens, apps, social media, or unsupervised friendships. We hand our children keys to a digital world filled with predators, unrealistic images, and toxic messaging, and we do so without healthy boundaries.

As parents, we're called to protect, not just physically, but emotionally and spiritually. That means creating boundaries around technology, relationships, and time. Not from a place of fear, but from a place of love.

You wouldn't give your child keys to a car without first teaching them how to drive. Don't give them digital freedom without the same intentional training. Set up filters. Monitor devices. Have ongoing conversations. Build trust through accountability, not blind permission.

Boundaries aren't about control; they're about care.

Remember ....

Our kids aren't just small people to manage. They are souls entrusted to us. And in the chaos of life, whether we're thriving or surviving, our calling remains the same:

to create a space of love, availability, safety, and respect.

Connection, consistency, and presence shape not just their childhood, but their future. They mold the framework for faith, relationships, and identity.

As you reflect on your parenting today, ask:

- Do my children know they are loved, even when they mess up?

- Do they see unity in our marriage?

- Do they feel safe emotionally, physically, and spiritually?

- Do they know that I will pick up the phone?

Build a home where your children can say, with confidence, *"Yes! I am loved; I am safe, and I matter."*

That is the kind of home that reflects God's heart and prepares your children to reflect His love to the world.

The Gift of Sideliners: Mentors and Safe Adults in Our Children's Lives

Why Our Voice Isn't Enough

As parents, it's tempting to believe that our children only need *our* advice and guidance. We'd like to think that our words are the strongest influence and our presence is enough to shape who they become. But the reality is, it simply isn't true.

Our kids live in a world of constant input. Their devices feed them voices every moment of the day: What is TikTok saying about who they should be? What does AI suggest about a hard question they're facing? Should they follow the influencers everyone else seems to follow, and should they adopt their worldview?

The truth is, it's impossible to be the *only* voice in your child's life. That's why one of the most important decisions we can make as parents is to intentionally surround our children with other safe, trusted adults who can stand alongside them. These people become extra pillars of support, voices of wisdom, shoulders to cry on, and examples of faith lived out in everyday life.

Who Are the Sideliners?

I call these trusted adults "sideliners."

For my girls, their sideliner team has been made up of women I trust. Women rooted in their own relationships with the Lord. Women who have proven faithful in their own walk. These are the ones who have chosen to show up on the sidelines of my children's lives.

Sometimes that has meant physically being there at events and milestones. Other times, it has looked like sending encouraging texts, cheering them on before a big test, mentoring them through career decisions, or hosting them in their homes with love and generosity. Each sideliner has invested in my daughters in unique ways, but all have carried the same message: *"You matter. I see you. I'm here for you."*

My daughters know they each have a handful of women they can call, day or night, if they need something, and if for any reason my husband, Gregg, or I are not the ones they choose to call. What an absolute gift this is!

Why Sideliners Matter

When another adult chooses to invest in your child, it carries a powerful message:

"I believe in you. You are valuable; not because I have to love you, but because I choose to love you."

That message sinks deep into the heart of a young person. It gives them an expanded sense of belonging and security. It reinforces that they are seen, cared for, and worth someone's time and attention. And in a culture where the digital world can so easily distort identity, sideliner voices bring truth, balance, and encouragement.

Your Call as a Parent and Friend

So here's the challenge: **make this a priority.** Don't leave it up to chance. Invite and encourage safe adults into your child's world. Cultivate these relationships. Give your kids permission to turn to them.

And just as importantly – be a sideliner for the children of your closest friends. Step into their lives with encouragement, prayer, and presence. Stand on the sidelines of their story and remind them that they matter.

This role is life-changing. It doesn't require perfection, just consistency, care, and the willingness to invest.

1. What are some practical ways you can build a deeper emotional connection with your child this week?
2. How might being more emotionally available change the way your child experiences love and security in your home?
3. In what areas of parenting could greater consistency, or more unity between you and your spouse, bring a stronger sense of safety to your children?
4. What boundaries might need to be established or revisited to protect your child's emotional, spiritual, or physical well-being?
5. Who are the current sideliners in your child's life?

CHAPTER 21

Stepping In and Stepping Up: A Call to Men in the Family

When I was thinking about this parenting chapter I knew how important it was to add special emphasis on the father's role in the home. I have been incredibly blessed, because I grew up with a father who was so intentional, involved, connected and loving. I then was lucky enough to marry a man who is equally so with our own 3 children. So I asked my amazing husband Gregg to write about his perspective of the role of the father and am so incredibly excited to have you hear from him directly! So here he is ....

The Cultural Narrative: The Passive Dad

Let's be honest, there's a narrative our culture keeps pushing, and it's not doing anyone any favors. If you flip through TV channels or scroll through your favorite sitcoms, what picture do you see of dads? The dopey father, clueless and passive. The man who's just along for the ride while mom runs the house, raises the kids, and holds the emotional reins.

And for a long time, I bought into that. Maybe not consciously, but practically, I lived it. I thought I was doing my part. I went to work, provided for my family, and tried to be available when needed. But somewhere along the way, I stopped leading. I stopped stepping in fully, and I started coasting.

What I didn't realize is that coasting communicates something very loud and clear: "You've got this, so I won't step in."

That message isn't fair to our wives. It's not fair to our kids. And it's definitely not the call God gives us as men.

The Hidden Struggle: "She's So Controlling"

I've sat with countless men in crisis, men whose marriages are breaking or have already broken, and one of the most common refrains I hear is this: "My wife is just so controlling."

She controls the kids, the schedule, the finances. "I feel like I can't lead. There's no room for me."

But here's the hard truth: most of the time, she didn't take control because she wanted to rule over everything. She took control because *someone had to*.

When I looked at my own marriage through that lens, I had to ask a painful but necessary question: **Was I really leading?**

Not just having good intentions. Not just saying the right things. Was I actually showing up with consistency, vision, courage, and care?

The answer, for a long time, was no.

Leadership Means Showing Up

Let's redefine leadership in the home. It isn't domination. It isn't being the loudest voice. It isn't demanding the final say.

Real leadership is servanthood. Initiative. Consistency. Emotional presence. It's the courage to make hard decisions instead of avoiding them. It's leaning into tough conversations rather than brushing them aside. It's leading with purpose and heart—seeking God, taking responsibility, and keeping the long-term health of your marriage and family as the central focus.

Leadership means:

- Taking ownership of the emotional and spiritual tone of your home.

- Making decisions in partnership with your wife.

- Being available to your kids, not just physically, but mentally and emotionally.

- Checking in, showing up, stepping up, leaning in, even when you're tired.

This isn't about being perfect. It's about being **present**.

Shared Responsibility: This Is OUR Job

Men, here's a reality we must embrace: parenting and leading our homes is a *shared* responsibility.

It's not a favor we do for our wives. It's not a job we're helping them with. It's our calling too.

Some of us work long hours. Some of us run businesses. Some of us are on the road. And yes, your work is important. But while we are gone and when we come home, our job doesn't end.

- Can you send a supportive text during the day?

- Can you check in with her schedule and plan to help?

- Can you ask, "What can I take off your plate this week?"

The emotional load your wife carries is real - and often invisible. If she's been with the kids all day, you're not walking into a spa when you get home. You're stepping onto a battlefield. And your family needs you in it and leading the charge.

Humor and History: A 1950s Snapshot

To lighten the moment, and maybe to show how far we've come, let's take a peek into the past. I came across what was supposedly a 1950s home economics guide for young wives. It offered advice to wives for when their husbands arrive home, like:

- Have dinner ready and waiting.

- Touch up your makeup and be cheerful.

- Quiet the children and tidy the home.

- Greet your husband with a smile.

- Never complain if he's late or goes out without you.

- Make the evening all about him.

It's laughable now (and maybe terrifying), but it reveals something about the cultural expectations we once had, and how extreme the pendulum has swung.

But let's not swing the pendulum too far the other way. The solution isn't for men to dominate completely. It's to step into *shared responsibility* with humility, awareness, intentionality, action, and love.

The Real Question: How Do We Show Up?

So let's flip the script.

What if *you* were the one bringing positive energy into the house at the end of the day?

What if instead of needing your wife to be your emotional refuge, you stepped into the door and became *hers*?

- Can you let go of the stress of work before you walk in?

- Can you bring laughter into the house?

- Can you notice her exhaustion before you demand relief for your own?

These are questions I ask myself daily. Not because I'm naturally great at it, but because I *need* the reminder. We are called to love like Christ, who didn't come to be served, but to serve.

That kind of leadership changes a home.

The Challenge: Step Up, Don't Check Out

So men, here's the challenge:

Don't check out. Don't believe the lie that you're just along for the ride. Your presence matters. Your leadership is needed.

Not perfect leadership. Not loud leadership. Not domineering leadership.

But steady, humble, servant-hearted, Christ-centered leadership.

Be fully present. Be action oriented. You're not just a passenger in your family. You've been given the wheel.

So grab it. Drive with purpose. And lead with love.

A Higher Calling: Offering Love Humble Authority and Servant Leadership

When we talk about leadership in the home, it can be tempting to think in terms of authority, control, or even status. But Jesus paints a radically different picture: *"Whoever wants to become great among you must be your servant... just as the Son of Man did not come to be served, but to serve, and to give his life as a ransom for many"* (Matthew 20:26–28).

This isn't just an ideal – it's a model. And it's not theoretical; it's deeply practical.

We aren't just here to perform roles or to project strength. We're here to reflect Christ's heart. Especially for men, what greater example could we follow than Jesus Himself, who led with compassion, humility, and sacrifice?

1 Corinthians 16:13-14 puts it this way: *"Be watchful, stand firm in the faith, act like men, be strong. Let all that you do be done in love."*

And this isn't about abandoning your dreams or passions. Jesus had a mission. He lived with purpose and intention, but He always folded that mission into His love and service for others. So the question is: what would our homes look like if we followed His lead? If we laid down our lives – not literally, but sacrificially, to serve and build up our wives and children, to be deeply rooted in our faith, to be strong, to act like men, and to do everything in love?

Living With Purpose

There is a quiet lie many men begin to believe as they seek to love and serve their families: that doing so requires the slow surrender of their own dreams and passions. That in order to support the calling of their wife and children, they must fade quietly into the background. In the shadows, a man can begin to glaze over - his fire dimming, his identity blurring - until a subtle, inward death sets in.

But the truth is exactly the opposite.

You were created on purpose and for a purpose. Before you took your first breath, the God of the universe saw you, knew you, and formed you with intention. He gave you a unique identity, a specific role to play, and a mission to live out. The dreams and passions you carry were not accidents or distractions - they were planted in you by God Himself.

One of the greatest gifts you can give your wife and children is not self-erasure, but a man fully alive. A man grounded in who God has called him to be. A man pursuing the mission God has set before him with clarity, humility, and conviction.

To abandon that calling; to live with dulled vision, a fading sense of identity, and a quiet resignation - is not loving leadership. It does not strengthen a family; it weakens it. If you find yourself unsure of your calling or uncertain of who God created you to be, spend time with Him and ask. He knows. And He desires for you to know. He placed that purpose uniquely within you.

A man who lives fully in his God-given identity, who passionately pursues the life and mission God designed for him, is a man on fire. That fire does not consume his family, it warms them. It stirs his wife and children to discover and pursue their own callings. A man alive in his purpose is better equipped to lead, to love, and to serve well.

So as you pour into your family and humbly serve them, do not shrink back. Step forward with courage. Live out the mission and purpose you were uniquely created for, because your family doesn't need you to disappear. They need you fully present, fully alive, and fully engaged in the calling God placed on your life.

Providing: More Than a Paycheck

We often hear the term "provider" and immediately think of financial responsibility. While that is certainly part of the equation, Scripture offers a broader vision:

"Anyone who does not provide for their relatives, and especially for their own household, has denied the faith and is worse than an unbeliever." 1 Timothy 5:8

That's intense. But providing isn't only about bringing home a paycheck. It's about presence. It's about structure, safety, guidance, and love. Some fathers are so focused on financial provision that they're emotionally and physically absent. Others are ever-present but neglect the practical needs of their families - jobless, unfocused, or disengaged.

True provision involves **balance**, and balance is hard. Some seasons require hustle, sacrifice, and grit. Others call us to slow down, connect, and recalibrate. The extremes - for extended or indefinite periods of time - whether overwork or passivity, can be damaging. Healthy provision is holistic: spiritual, emotional, financial, and physical.

Leading Spiritually: The Invisible Legacy

"Fathers, do not exasperate your children; instead, bring them up in the training and instruction of the Lord." Ephesians 6:4

For many men, spiritual leadership feels awkward or even overwhelming. Maybe you don't know where to start. Maybe your own walk with God feels shaky. Maybe you feel unqualified.

You're not alone in that.

There are men in your community and church – mentors, friends, discipleship leaders – who want to walk with you. Don't carry this alone. Lean into brothers in the faith. Find encouragement, accountability, and practical wisdom.

Just get started, even if it's in small ways. Pray with your kids. Pray for your wife. Let them see you in the Word. It doesn't need to be polished or perfect. It just needs to be real.

Let your children hear you say things like, *"This is a hard moment, but let's ask God what He thinks,"* or *"Here's a verse that's helped me through something like this."* You're guiding and discipling your children not just with words, but with your life.

And remember that your wife is your greatest ministry, before your kids and before your church.

Ministering to Your Wife: The First Step in Family Leadership

Start there. Start with her.

Spiritual leadership doesn't mean preaching sermons at home. It means **creating space**. Giving her time for rest. Protecting her time with God. Knowing what she needs – not in a distant or checklist way, but with humility and intentionality.

Ask yourself:

- Is my wife spiritually well?

- Does she feel supported?

- Have I made room for her to grow and thrive?

When husbands and wives are united spiritually, everything else flows from that. You may not have all the parenting answers, but your children will see the way you treat one another. That foundation of unity and love preaches louder than any lesson.

A Prayer for Fathers

Pastor Rob Rienow once said, *"The number one reason why God made me was to minister to this woman [my wife]."* He encouraged men to pray a simple prayer daily:

"God, turn my heart to the ministry of my wife."

It's short, but it's transformational.

Because without a heart change, leadership becomes a burden. And your family will feel it. But when your heart is softened by God, you lead from grace, not obligation. Even if your wife is spiritually ahead of you. Even if you feel unworthy. Remember: Christ is the only One who can help you rise to this high calling. You don't need to lower the standard. You need to ask Him to lift you up.

Prioritizing Your Family: Living What You Believe

Your children are always watching.

They notice how you spend your time. How you speak to your wife. How you handle stress. How you live out your faith.

So be present. Coach their games. Show up at their events. Put the phone down and tune in. Every moment matters. Decide to be intentional. Start conversations – even small ones. Initiate an activity. Simply ask about their day and their friends. Ask about their thoughts and their opinions. Sometimes all you need to do is listen.

And never underestimate the power of your words. Support your wife *in front* of your children. Tell them how beautiful, strong, and amazing their mom is. Let them hear you cheer for her. "Who's got the best mom in the world?" is a fun way to get them involved, but it also builds a culture of honor and unity in the home.

On the flip side, constant criticism, sarcasm, or tension creates insecurity in kids. If you want them to respect their mom, show them how it's done. If you want them to pursue faith, let them see it alive in you.

Conclusion: The Gospel at Home

In all of this – serving, providing, leading, loving – the goal isn't perfection. The goal is surrender.

No man is enough on his own. None of us have what it takes in our own strength to lead a family with faith and love. But we do have access to the One who does.

So kneel often. Ask for wisdom. Invite Christ to lead you first so you can lead your family well.

Let your home be a place where the Gospel is lived out, tested, and experienced - not just spoken. Where humility, sacrifice, presence, engagement and love are the foundation stones. Where your children grow up knowing what it means to follow Jesus, understand who he is, and why it matters - not because of what you said, but because of how you lived and by seeing what Jesus has done in your life.

The War Room: Fighting for Your Family

Building a Home Where Christ Reigns and Warriors Rise

As parents, spouses, and followers of Christ, we face a daily tension: the push and pull between our work ambitions and our family priorities. In a culture that often glorifies hustle over home, achievement over attachment, we must ask ourselves:

Are we willing to lose a little at work in order to win at home?

It's not about shirking responsibility or letting go of excellence. It's about making conscious, courageous choices that honor our deepest values. Maybe we won't get the next promotion or recognition. Maybe we won't work those extra hours. But what we gain in return when being present, connected, and committed to our family is a victory far more eternal.

Christ calls us to something deeper. **He calls us to reorder our lives around what truly matters.** And that means our marriage, our children, our family, come just after Him - not after our careers, not after our comfort, not after our image.

As mentioned previously, this doesn't mean shrinking back or fading away from the purpose God created us for. We are called to live fully in the mission God has placed on our lives. Both are possible. We can pursue a clear calling and purpose—often lived out through our work—while also leading and guiding our family well. In fact, both are critical. You do have a mission to live out as you seek God. But if your family is slowly breaking or being left behind as you push forward, it's worth taking a hard look at whether that calling is truly from God or whether it has drifted into something self-seeking.

One practical way to guard against this is to bring your family into the journey with you. Invite them into the story and the process. Communicate clearly what God has placed on your heart—what He has called you into, and the purpose and passion behind what you do, including your work. Help them understand why it matters. Let them ask questions and engage with it. When you do this, your spouse and children don't feel sidelined by your mission—they become part of it. They become your biggest cheerleaders, and they get to walk alongside you and live the mission with you, instead of feeling left behind.

Open Communication: Asking, Listening, Connecting

One of the most overlooked tools of parenting is also one of the simplest: conversation. Especially for fathers, it can feel awkward or unnatural to initiate open dialogue with our children. But connection doesn't always require deep, emotional speeches. Sometimes, it starts with a story.

Tell your children about your own life – your childhood, their grandparents, the silly things you did growing up, the lessons you learned. These stories become seeds that blossom into connection. They create an entry point into conversation and into the hearts of your kids.

Ask intentional questions:

- What do you love that I do for you?

- What would you love to do with me?

- What's something you wish we did more?

Take your kids out one-on-one. Grab some ice cream. Go for a walk. Ride bikes. Sit in the grass. Sit on the edge of their bed at night and listen about their day and their worries. The point isn't the event. It's the access. The space to talk and be heard.

When we guess what our kids need, we often get it wrong. But when we ask and listen, they'll tell us the truth. They're honest. They're brave. And they're longing for our attention more than our perfection.

Be a Warrior for Your Family

The world needs warriors. Not just in boardrooms or battlefields, but in **living rooms and kitchens and kids' bedrooms**. Warriors who rise not to dominate, but to protect. Not to rule, but to love.

Men, we are called to be those warriors. **Christ first. Then your spouse. Then your children.** That's the order of battle. And it is a battle.

It's not always glamorous. There will be days you don't feel like showing up. Days when your marriage is rocky. Days when your kids feel like strangers. Maybe your children are grown and the damage seems too great. But warriors don't walk off the battlefield. **They get back up. They stay. They fight. They heal.**

If you chose to marry, if you chose to have children, then build your life around that family, with **Christ at the center**. Dream big dreams. Pursue your calling. But ask yourself: *Is this building up my family? Is this protecting them? Is this drawing us closer together under God's mission for our lives?*

Write a family mission statement. Review it often. Let it direct your career decisions, your financial priorities, and your time commitments.

Honored to Live Life With You

One of my favorite movies is "300". In the film, there's a powerful scene at the end, after a defeating battle, where the warrior king Leonidas lies dying. His comrade says, "I am honored to die beside you." And Leonidas replies, "I was honored to live beside you." As he breathes his last, he calls out with passion and love: *"My queen, my wife, my love."*

What if we framed our lives that way?

What if, in the midst of the battles – financial stress, parenting challenges, marital conflict – we could look at our family and say, *"It is my honor to live life with you. To fight **for** you and beside you. To sacrifice for you. To give my all for you."*

True strength is not just surviving the fight. **It's choosing to love through it.**

Thank you for listening. Let's be men who step up, who stand firm in the faith, who act like men, who are strong. Let's be men that do all things in love.

And now I will hand it back to my wife :)

A Wife's Perspective: Let Him Lead

As women, many of us long for a warrior, someone who will stand in the gap, take up the shield, and fight for the family. But sometimes, in the absence of that, we pick up the sword ourselves. We become the leader, the protector, the planner, the fighter. Not because we want to, but because we feel like we have to.

But I had to learn: **I wasn't designed to be a warrior.** I was designed to be led by one, to help and work alongside him with my unique roles and purpose.

When I stepped back and made room for my husband to lead, he stepped forward. Not perfectly, but faithfully. And now, every day, he chooses to be a warrior for our family.

Wives, this doesn't mean silencing your voice. It means making space for your husband. It means choosing to believe in him again. It means giving him room to rise. It means giving him respect and showing belief in him.

Husbands, if your wife does that, then **rise. Lead. Love. Protect.** Not with domination, but with grace. Not with control, but with humility.

Parenting with the Gospel in Mind

The Gospel reframes how we parent. It gives us a foundation of grace and truth that changes everything.

1. **We are all children.**
   We don't have to be perfect parents. We're children of God, still learning, growing, repenting. Let your kids see that. Let them see you depend on your perfect Father.

2. **We are equal.**
   Parent and child, yes, but also brother and sister in Christ. Equal in worth. Adopted by God. United in the race of faith.

3. **We are forgiven.**
   Our limitations don't disqualify us. Our mistakes don't define us. We rest in God's forgiveness, and we extend that same grace to our kids.

4. **We belong.**
   Our value doesn't come from performance

but from Christ. And our children need that truth. They need to know their worth is unshakable.

5. **We are called to obedience.**
   The first law we obey is to love the Lord our God. That love flows into our parenting. It gives us the courage to lead with both conviction and compassion.

Redeeming the Room

Just like we redecorate our children's bedrooms over time, **our parenting must constantly adapt**. Today it's princess posters. Tomorrow it's music posters and mood swings. And one day, the bunk beds will be gone.

But if we've poured love and time and truth into that room, it becomes sacred.

So build something lasting.

Whether your children are toddlers or teens, still at home or already grown, **the war isn't over.** There's still a battle worth fighting. There's still healing to be found. There's still enough grace to redeem the story.

Because when Christ leads our home, and we choose to follow, **we don't just survive. We build legacies.**

Chapter 21 *Reflection Questions:*

1. In what ways have you seen or experienced the "passive dad" narrative in your own life or culture, and how does it compare to the servant-hearted, Christ-centered leadership described in this chapter?

2. Reflect on your current role in your family: are there areas where you've been coasting instead of leading with presence, intentionality, humility, and love? What first steps could you take to change that?

3. How can you begin, or deepen, the practice of spiritual leadership in your home, even if it feels awkward or unfamiliar? What might this look like on a practical, daily level?

4. Think about your relationship with your spouse. How can you create more space for their spiritual, emotional, and personal well-being while building unity in your marriage?

5. This chapter calls men to be "warriors" for their families, fighting for connection, faith, and love. What is one specific battle you feel called to fight for your family right now, and how will you rely on Christ for strength in it?

Part 7

DINING ROOM
&
GUEST ROOM

Chapter 22

Recognizing the Role of Each Friend in Your Life

Friendship has always been one of my favorite topics, partly because it has shaped so much of who I am today. From a young age, I understood that people matter, that relationships require intentionality, and that the way we invest in others deeply influences the story of our lives.

But here's what I didn't understand for far too long: not all friendships are meant to carry the same weight, and more friends doesn't always mean deeper connection. I used to think a long list of people to call for a coffee date or girls' night somehow validated my worth. I stretched myself thin, determined to make time for everyone, whether they had been in my life for fifteen years or fifteen days. I felt guilty for missed birthdays, worried that choosing to spend time with one person instead of the whole group made me disloyal, and often prioritized acquaintances over moments with Gregg or the girls.

Eventually, I had to face a hard truth: my view of friendship needed a total renovation.

In this chapter, we explore the "Dining Room" and the "Guest Room" of your relational home – what they both represent and why every marriage needs both.

The Power of Friendship and Accountability

As believers, we are not called to walk alone. Marriage is designed to be a partnership, but even a strong marriage doesn't thrive in isolation. We need community. We need safe friendships. We need accountability.

The Bible speaks often and clearly about the role of friendship in our lives. In fact, healthy friendships are often used by God to refine, encourage, and mature us. But not every friendship serves the same purpose.

Defining Biblical Friendship

The Bible doesn't shy away from defining the kind of friends we need. Here are key characteristics of a true friend:

1. **Loves at all times**
   Proverbs 17:17 – "A friend loves at all times."
   A true friend isn't seasonal. They stick around in sunshine and in storms.
2. **Speaks hard truths**
   Proverbs 27:6 – "Wounds from a friend can be trusted."
   Sometimes love means confrontation. Accountability stings, but it heals.
3. **More loyal than family**
   Proverbs 18:24 – "There is a friend who sticks closer than a brother."
   True friends become spiritual family.

4. **Sharpens and challenges you**
    Proverbs 27:17 – "As iron sharpens iron, so one man sharpens another."
    Growth happens in friction, when friends don't let you stay stuck.

5. **Gives wise counsel**
    Proverbs 13:20 – "He who walks with the wise grows wise."
    The wisdom of your friends will either lift you up or pull you down.

6. **Sacrifices for you**
    John 15:13 – "Greater love has no one than this, that he lay down his life for his friends."
    Love in action is costly – and rare.

7. **Leads you toward God**
    Colossians 3:16 – "Teach and admonish one another... with gratitude in your hearts to God."
    Spiritual friendship points you to worship, not just sympathy.

The Dining Room: Friendship and Fellowship

Think about the dining room. It's where we host others, serve meals, share stories, and enjoy each other's company. It's polished. The lights are on. The table is set. It's the part of your home that most people see, and it's a great place to build connections.

Dining Room friends are the social friends in our lives. You might grab dinner together, catch up after church, or enjoy a weekend outing. These are people who bring joy, offer companionship, and walk alongside you in the everyday rhythms of life.

These relationships matter. We need people who help us laugh, help us celebrate, and help us relax. These friendships also function as bridges – many "guest room" friendships start in the dining room. The key is to recognize their role: they aren't always the people who know your deepest struggles, but they play a valuable role in keeping your heart encouraged and your life grounded in community.

You can, and should, have many dining room friends, as a couple and individually. They bring vitality to your social life and can often be a source of refreshing.

Take a moment and think about the friendships in your own life: the people who have been woven into your story during different seasons. For me, many of them have come as a result of parenting. They were the moms in my playgroup, the ones I sat next to on the sidelines of soccer games, lacrosse matches, tennis tournaments, and volleyball courts. (Can you tell I logged a lot of hours watching my kids play sports?)

They were the moms on the PTO with me, planning school events, organizing fundraisers, and volunteering for anything that needed an extra set of hands. As couples, these friends gathered at our house for game nights or joined us for pizza by the community pool while the kids swam until dark.

When I think back on those years, my mind plays a reel of laughter, conversations, and countless ordinary moments that became anything but ordinary because we shared them together. These friendships carried me through the chaos of raising kids, and honestly, I don't know how I would have survived the early years without them.

Intentionality in the "Dining Room"

Once you begin to see your friendships with greater clarity and understand the categories they fall into it brings a surprising sense of freedom. You no longer feel the weight of trying to pour the same amount of energy into every single relationship. In fact, you realize that doing so can leave you drained and even negatively affect your marriage and family.

There is beauty in enjoying your "dining room" friendships for what they are. These relationships matter deeply. They give you people to laugh with, share experiences with, and enjoy lighter conversations with, without the pressure of constant connection. It's okay if you're not calling these friends weekly to check on their kids or asking for their advice on your biggest life decisions. A few of these relationships may naturally grow into "guest room" friendships over time, but let that happen on its own. Don't force it.

Authenticity in these friendships doesn't mean you have to share every vulnerability. Sitting on the sidelines of a volleyball game isn't always the right moment to pour out your heart about your marriage. Watching your kids crawl around a playgroup isn't necessarily the time to give or seek deep parenting advice.

We often confuse authenticity with vulnerability, but they aren't the same thing. Authenticity simply means you are showing up as your true self without hiding behind a mask or pretending to be someone you're not. And that's what makes "dining room" friendships so life-giving – they allow you to be real without demanding every part of you.

1. Think about the friendships in your life right now. Who are the people that bring joy, laughter, and companionship – your "dining room" friends? How do they add vitality to your life and marriage?

2. Are there relationships where you feel obligated to invest the same energy into every interaction? How does this affect your time, emotional well-being, or marriage?

3. Reflect on the friendships that have shaped your story over the years. Which friendships have carried you through seasons of challenge or celebration? How did they impact your personal growth or your family life?

4. Consider the difference between authenticity and vulnerability. In your dining room friendships, how can you show up as your true self without feeling pressure to share every struggle or personal detail?

Chapter 23

Guest Room: Mentorship and Accountability

Now think about the guest room. This is a space that is rarely perfect, but deeply personal. When someone stays in your guest room, they see the behind-the-scenes. They witness the early morning unfiltered version of your life. They might see the mess, the laundry, the stress.

Guest room friends (or even extended family members) are your inner circle. These are the mentors, accountability partners, and confidants who know both your highlights and your hardships. They've seen you at your best and worst, and they're still there. **These people have earned the right to speak truth into your life.**

(On a side note, I would like to point out that for some people, extended family is able to be classified in this way, and for others, it's not possible. What differentiates this space is that these are the people - whether friends or family - that you allow to have a strong voice in your life. So, for many of you, you might deal with complexities of strained relationships with family or even long-time friends. There are many factors that would go into making boundary decisions regarding actual time spent with them, but where you can set a very definite boundary is the influence they have in the decisions you make in your life. So know that this chapter is for those

people who you allow to influence your life, to speak into your life, and to hold you accountable)

You likely only have a few guest room friends in your life. Depth doesn't require quantity. These are the people you must intentionally pursue, protect, and invite into your spiritual and emotional life. They're the ones who will challenge your blind spots and stand beside you through storms.

And as couples, it's important to nurture shared guest room friendships – other couples you trust, learn from, and grow with.

When I think about my handful of "guest room" friends, tears well up in my eyes. The gratitude I feel for them, and the impact they've had on my life and marriage, runs so deep that I sometimes wonder how I got so lucky.

When I close my eyes, I see a hundred reels of memories playing in my mind. They are filled with laughter, inside jokes, and countless shared experiences: beach trips and mountain getaways, birthday parties and baby showers, late nights in pajamas retelling the same stories until 3 a.m., laughing so hard we cried. We've celebrated each other's kids' accomplishments and been some of the first calls when exciting news came our way.

But what sets these friendships apart are the moments of profound depth. They're the friends who showed up when life felt impossible – the one who dropped everything and drove straight to my house when I was in crisis, staying as long as I needed. The one I call when I'm wrestling with parenting decisions because she knows my girls almost as well as I do. The one who brought meals and sat with me after back surgery, crying because she knew how hard it was for me not to pick up my kids.

They are the friends I can sit with on a quiet beach and share my deepest fears with. The ones who love me enough to call me out when my attitude needs a reset. They are the couples who chose authenticity over appearances, laying everything on the table in our living rooms, offering honesty, support, and accountability as we have sharpened each other's lives. They are the ones who walked with us through the hardest seasons of our marriage, who stood beside us when we recommitted to each other, fully understanding the miracle unfolding before them.

These friends believe in the best version of me, cheer me on relentlessly, and most importantly, point me to Jesus every single time, with love.

Understanding Your Why

Before inviting someone into your "guest room", ask yourself:
Why?

1. **Have I been selective?**
   Not every friendly person should be a close friend.
   Proverbs 22:24-25 warns against bonding

with a quick-tempered person, lest their ways become yours.

2. **Have I considered proximity?**
Proverbs 27:10 reminds us that a nearby neighbor is often more helpful than a distant relative. Relationships thrive when there's shared space, time, and values. This basis can then carry friendship into the rest of your life – but the shared time builds the foundation. Some of my closest friends no longer live in the same area – but our friendship began in the same location with shared memories. These friendships have remained close because our values are still aligned regardless of distance.

3. **Have I set boundaries?**
Healthy friendships respect time, emotional space, and relational health. Not everyone gets full access to your heart, and that's not unkind; it's wise.

4. **Do we have mutuality?**
Friendship is a two-way street. Laugh together. Cry together. Challenge each other. There should be shared interests and accountability.

5. **Is there mutual respect?**
Watch how they speak when you're not around, and how you speak of them too. *Proverbs 16:28* says gossip separates close friends.

6. **Do we speak truth, not just comfort?**
Proverbs 28:23 tells us honest rebuke is

better than flattery. If your friends only tell you what you want to hear, it might be time to go deeper or reassess.

7. **Can we forgive quickly?**
   Proverbs 17:9 – "He who covers over an offense promotes love."
   Friendships endure when forgiveness is frequent.

The Intentionality of "Guest Room" Friendships.

When I think about what it takes to be intentional in your closest friendships, I realize it touches on nearly every chapter of this book. The same values, disciplines, and processes you've applied to your marriage or family relationships also apply here.

For those few trusted friends who speak truth into your life, consider these questions and reminders to guide you as you nurture those connections:

A. Foundation (Is God your common core?)

- Is God the center of their life?
- Is your compass the same?
- Is your priority of the foundation in your life the same?

B. Bathroom (Seeing behind the mask)

- Do you understand each other's masks and call each other out when you are not being authentic?

- Do you understand each other's history and
  what got you to where you are today
- Do you know each other's greatest fears?
- Do you know each other's triggers?

C. Bedroom (Communication)

- Are you a ready listener?
- Are you slow to speak?
- Do you speak about topics like your faith,
  marriage, ministry, parenting, work, career,
  and health?
- Do you do Emotional Strategic Planning with
  each other?
- Do you ask each other to define needs?

D. Family Room (The Heart)

- Do you know the heart of your friend's life?
- Do you know their view on family, and does
  it align with your view of family?
- Do you know the emotional climate of their
  home and what they hope their home
  represents?

E. Kids Room (Parenting)

- Do you know their view on parenting - and
  even if you have different styles, that you are
  able to respect each other because your core
  "why" behind what you do is the same?

F. Office (Work Life)

- Do you know their work goals?

- Do you know their passions?

Friendship Boundaries in Marriage

Here's a vital reminder: **Your closest confidants should never be with the opposite sex (outside of family).** Even when intentions are pure, emotional intimacy with someone who isn't your spouse will sow division or confusion in your marriage.

Protect your marriage by setting clear rules around workplace friendships, digital communication, and vulnerable conversations. Be proactive, not reactive.

Also, make space for your spouse to develop individual friendships **guilt free.** Encourage them to spend time with their godly friends, have fun, and be refreshed.

Pursuing Accountability

You'll never stumble into accountability. You have to **pursue** it.

- Ask someone to walk with you spiritually.
- Invite challenge, not just comfort.
- Be willing to expose your weaknesses.
- Give permission for follow-up, not just venting.

Accountability is only powerful when it's regular, honest, and welcomed.

Friendship as a Spiritual Discipline

In a culture of curated images and surface-level connection, deep friendship is countercultural and Christlike.

God designed us for communion with Him and with others. In a healthy marriage, strong individual and couple friendships become a source of growth, encouragement, and mission. You aren't just maintaining friendships;you're cultivating a garden that reflects the heart of God.

So clean off the dining table. Make up the guest room. And invite those God has placed in your life in to walk with you in joy, truth, and grace.

1. Who are the few people in your life that you truly allow to speak truth into your life and hold you accountable – your "guest room" friends? How have they influenced your growth spiritually, emotionally, or relationally?

2. Before inviting someone into your inner circle, have you intentionally considered their character, values, and alignment with God's priorities? How do you ensure mutuality, respect, and honesty in these friendships?

3. How do you balance closeness with accountability while maintaining healthy boundaries, especially in friendships outside your marriage? Are there adjustments needed to protect your marriage and family?

4. Reflecting on the different "rooms" of friendship (Foundation, Bathroom, Bedroom, Family Room, Kids Room, Office), which areas of connection with your closest friends are strong, and where could you grow in depth and understanding?

5. Are you actively pursuing accountability in your life, or do you rely on chance? What steps can you take to invite trusted friends to challenge, encourage, and walk alongside you regularly?

Part 8

THE OFFICE

Chapter 24

The Office

Finding Balance in a Culture of Yes

Step into your office for a moment. Not the literal one with a desk and computer, but the space in your life where responsibilities pile up, tasks demand attention, and the clock seems to always be ticking. The "office" represents our sense of duty, productivity, and ambition. It's where we say "yes" to more work, more commitments, more obligations and, often, at a very steep cost.

We live in a culture of "yes." If there's a need, we meet it. If there's an opportunity, we chase it. If there's a request, we respond to it. At first glance, it may feel noble, even spiritual. But somewhere in the rush of <u>doing</u>, we begin to lose sight of <u>being</u>.

Let's look honestly at what we tend to say "yes" to:

- **More Work** – There's always more money to be made, more promotions to chase, more boxes to check.
- **More Ministry** – The needs are never-ending. It feels almost wrong to say no.
- **More Activities** – There's always another team to join, another group to lead, another calendar square to fill.
- **More Social Commitments** – We want to stay connected, relevant, liked.

Each "yes" can seem small on its own, but cumulatively, these choices can suffocate what matters most.

The Hidden Cost of Overcommitment

As we build our resumes and social calendars, something quieter begins to erode:

- Our **relationship with God** becomes a checkbox, not a lifeline.
- Our **marriage** turns into a business partnership rather than a haven.
- Our **family** gets the leftovers of our time and energy.
- Our **physical health** declines under the pressure.
- Our **friendships** become shallow or forgotten.
- Our **rest** becomes nonexistent, replaced with caffeine and anxiety.

We weren't made for this. And deep down, we know it.

Why Do We Say "Yes"?

To find freedom, we must first uncover our true motivations.

- **Identity** – We believe what we do defines who we are.
- **Acceptance** – We think if we do enough, people will approve of us.

- **Respect** – We want to be admired, to feel important.
- **Obligation** – We feel like we can't say no.
- **Expectation** – Everyone else is doing it, so we feel we should too.
- **Fear** – We hoard opportunities "just in case" tomorrow falls apart.
- **Money** – We chase financial stability or luxury, convinced it's never enough.

But what does God say about all of this?

The Truth About Our Identity

The truth is, your worth has never been about your output. God's Word anchors our identity in something unshakable:

- *"Even when we were dead in our trespasses, [He] made us alive together with Christ; by grace you have been saved."* (Ephesians 2:5)
- *"But God shows his love for us in that while we were still sinners, Christ died for us."* (Romans 5:8)
- *"See what kind of love the Father has given to us, that we should be called children of God; and so we are."* (1 John 3:1)

You are chosen. Loved. Valued. Not because of what you do, but because of who He is.

When we let false motivations drive our schedules, we serve idols – control, approval, security, money. But Scripture calls us to a better way:

- *"Keep your life free from love of money, and be content with what you have, for he has said, 'I will never leave you nor forsake you.'"* (Hebrews 13:5)

Acceptance, Respect, and Belonging

Do you know that you are fully accepted by God?

- *"But you are a chosen race, a royal priesthood, a holy nation, a people for his own possession..."* (1 Peter 2:9)
- *"Before I formed you in the womb I knew you..."* (Jeremiah 1:5)
- *"I have called you friends..."* (John 15:15)

The world's applause fades, but God's acceptance is eternal. We don't have to earn what's already been freely given.

The Call to Balance

Balance is not a myth. It's a spiritual discipline.

- *"For everything there is a season, and a time for every matter under heaven..."* (Ecclesiastes 3:1)
- *"Do not be conformed to this world, but be transformed by the renewal of your mind..."* (Romans 12:2)
- *"A false balance is an abomination to the Lord, but a just weight is His delight."* (Proverbs 11:1)

Balance doesn't mean doing everything evenly; it means doing everything obediently. It means knowing what God is asking of you in this season and letting go of everything else.

Fear and Worry: The Root Beneath the Busyness

Much of our overcommitment is rooted in fear:

- Fear of being left behind.
- Fear of not being enough.
- Fear of letting someone down.
- Fear that things will fall apart if we stop.

God speaks directly to that fear:

- *"Fear not, for I am with you…"* (Isaiah 41:10)
- *"Do not be anxious about anything… and the peace of God… will guard your hearts."* (Philippians 4:6-7)
- *"God gave us a spirit not of fear but of power and love and self-control."* (2 Timothy 1:7)

A Practical Path Forward

Let's make this tangible. Here's how to begin rebuilding your "office" with purpose:

1. Figure Out the Balance in Your Life and Marriage

Sit down with your spouse. Take inventory of your weekly commitments. Ask: What restores us? What drains us? What honors God?

2. Understand Your "Why"

Be honest: Why are you saying yes? Is it fear, pride, guilt? Name it. Invite God to speak into it.

3. Make Christ the Center

Everything flows from Him. If your schedule doesn't leave space for Him, it's not aligned with Him.

4. Reorient Your Thinking

As the Dalai Lama once said:

"Man sacrifices his health in order to make money. Then he sacrifices money to recuperate his health. Then he is so anxious about the future that he does not enjoy the present... he dies having never really lived."

Don't let that be your story. Reclaim the present. Reclaim peace.

5. Set Goals and Know Your Non-Negotiables

Your marriage, your walk with God, your rest. These are not optional. Build your schedule around them, not the other way around.

6. Unite Around Your Purpose

You and your spouse are a team. Make decisions together. Pray together. Say yes or no together.

7. Remember: God's Way May Look Different

Slower. Simpler. Stranger. But more full of life.
You won't always be understood. That's okay.

Count the cost.
Choose what truly matters.
Build your life around God's priorities, not the world's.

Staying United Through Busy Seasons

There will be seasons when the time commitment to a work endeavor is high. Maybe you're pursuing a promotion, launching a new business, or chasing a dream that requires extra focus. The key is making this decision together as a couple: standing as a united team, supporting each other through the demands of these times.

For us, Gregg's entrepreneurial journey has often meant long hours and frequent travel. Those seasons haven't always easy. Yet, when we stayed aligned on the "why" behind the sacrifices and kept communicating about how to feel seen and loved despite the busyness, something unexpected happened: we grew closer. Rather than driving a wedge between us, those demanding times became opportunities to strengthen our marriage.

In the end, the "office" of your life will either serve as a place of burnout or a base of blessing. The choice is yours. God is not calling you to do more; He is calling you to be with Him more.

Let this be the season you clear out the clutter, say yes with wisdom, and live from a place of peace.

Chapter 24 *Reflection Questions:*

1. When you look at your current commitments, which ones bring life and align with God's priorities, and which ones feel driven by fear, pride, or the need for approval?
2. How has saying "yes" too often affected your relationship with God, your marriage, your family, and your own emotional or physical health?
3. In what ways do you need to reorient your identity around God's truth instead of your productivity, accomplishments, or other people's expectations?
4. What practical steps can you and your spouse take to stay on the same page during busy seasons, so that your marriage grows stronger rather than strained?
5. If your "office" represents your life's commitments, what needs to be cleared out or restructured so it can become a base of blessing instead of a source of burnout?

Note from the Author

Now that you've taken the time to walk through this journey of renovating your life, and hopefully begun putting many of these tools into practice - what matters most is staying aware. Growth isn't a one-time project. It's an ongoing process of noticing the areas that need attention and being willing to step back in with care.

Just like a home, life looks its freshest right after a renovation. But over time, small cracks can form, paint can fade, and parts that once felt strong may need reinforcement. Make it a habit to "check the rooms" every few months. When seasons change or your family dynamics shift, revisit the spaces that feel worn. Even rereading a single chapter can help you realign, refresh, and repair before little issues become big ones.

So enjoy the new paint. Celebrate the beauty of what's been restored. But keep your tools nearby. A well-lived life, like a well-loved home, stays strong not because it never needs work, but because someone keeps showing up to care for it.

With gratitude,
Lize Landis

ACKNOWLEDGEMENTS

*First and foremost, I am nothing without my Savior, **Jesus Christ**. His love, grace, and constant guidance are the compass directing every step I take. Everything in these pages begins and ends with Him.*

*To my husband **Gregg**, this book would not exist without you. Every tool, every process, and every example within these pages is tried and true because we have lived them side by side. Together, we have built each "room" of our life, faced seasons where we waited too long to renovate, and chosen the courage to rebuild. We practice checking in on every area not only because we believe deeply in the covenant of marriage, but because we believe in one another. There is not a single part of this book that we have not personally walked out. Your influence is woven into every chapter — your passion, dedication, faith, and love shaping the life we've built together. Thank you for leading our marriage with strength and humility, for making our family your highest priority, and for loving me so faithfully and well.*

*To my three incredible daughters, **Jaime, Katelyn, and Taylor** - to say I am grateful for our family is an understatement. I am at my very happiest when we are together. You are my greatest encouragers, my strongest supporters, and the motivation behind all that I do. I treasure every memory we've made and look forward to all the adventures still to come. I love you more than words can hold.*

*To my parents, **Mom and Dad** - you have always been my north star. Your marriage has been a living example of how to love well, stay committed, and build a family the right way. The sacrifices you've made for all of us can never be repaid. I am endlessly grateful to be your daughter. Mom, thank you for being the first to read this book and share your thoughtful input - your wisdom and insight meant more than you know.*

*To my sister, **Karen** - thank you for editing this book with such care and excellence. Your insight, wisdom, and attention to detail made every part of it better. The way you live with purpose & intentionality, continually learning and growing, and loving your girls so deeply inspires me every single day. You are the strongest person I know. I love you.*

*To my brother, **Renaut** - thank you for being a powerful example of what it means to continually turn back to Jesus. Your dedication to knowing His Word, your commitment to living with purpose, and your authenticity in walking out your faith - through both the highs and the lows - inspire me daily. I love you.*

*To my in-laws on both sides of our family - **Brooke; Karen & Ed; Vicki; Brian & Liga; and Charles & Eileen** - thank you for your constant love and support. Each of you has been an example through your faith, your devotion to one another, and your shared commitment to family. I love you and I am so grateful for all of you.*

*To my niece, **Dakota**, who used her incredible talents to design the cover of this book! Thank you so much!*

*To my "ride-or-die" friends - I am beyond blessed to have a circle of women who are truly chosen sisters. I can call any one of you at any hour, and you are there. You know me. You have walked through life with me - the beautiful seasons and the hardest ones. We have laughed together until we cried and cried together until we laughed. We have challenged one another in our marriages, supported each other as mothers, and stayed connected across every distance. I am who I am today because of your friendship. **Laurie L., Jaime J., Maile S., Jenn S., Lori B., Amy B., Jane H., Niesa P., and Summer D.** - thank you. I love you all!*

To the friends who have walked with me through different seasons of life - across schools, on sports sidelines, planning conferences, book clubs, playgroups, missional communities, PTSOs, and so many spaces in between - thank you. Each of you has left a meaningful mark on my life, and I am deeply grateful for the role you've played in my journey.

*A special thank you to **Summer** - your collaboration on this book, your ideas, edits, encouragement, wisdom, and steady support meant everything. I truly would not have finished it without you. I'm so grateful for your friendship and honored to work alongside you, especially through Marigold, as we continue pursuing the work God has placed before us. I can't wait to see how He uses this journey to impact lives together.*